The Science Club Handbook

The Science Club Handbook

THE COMPLETE BLUEPRINT FOR OPENING SCIENCE CLUB AT YOUR SCHOOL

● ● ●

Alan Small

ISBN-13: 9780692716779
ISBN-10: 0692716777
Library of Congress Control Number: 2016909328
Alan Small, Fort Worth, TX

Contents

Two young explorers boil water in a paper cup by playing with fire

My love and gratitude to the following folks:

To my parents for sleeping in parking lots, camping in the rain, supporting model-rocket and Hardy Boys habits, *buying* airline tickets, coaching sports teams, driving me to church, taking me hunting, giving me an awesome brother, and for agreeing to come back home after the missing snake was located. You guys are pretty stinkin' cool.

To my friends from the Fort Worth Museum of Science and History (FWMSH) for showing me how to have fun with *real* science—Irene Stemple, Karen Massey, Peggy Rush, and Nancy Lamb. I take *great* pleasure in remembering your talents as Museum School teachers. I love teaching, and any success I find in it is based on skills I learned from you. I strive to be like you when I'm in front of students.

Chip Lindsey, Jim Diffily, Bill Voss, and Colleen Blair, thank you for showing me how to enjoy truly wonderful science adventures without losing an eye, burning down the building, or getting sued.

Monta Noe, Cathy Barthelemy, Miki Gabbard, Amanda Morales, Lucy Hale, Leishawn Spotted Bear, Julie Cross-Steele, Kit Goolsby, Judy Ivey, Betsy Eudy, and Jeanie Wolfe, I look up to all of you as experts and friends I am blessed to have known.

Anne Herndon, I couldn't possibly compress the amount of respect I have for you into one sentence. I guess three will have to do. Watching you orchestrate and evolve your craft is inspiring.

Jonathon Mills, Saafir, Myles Hayes, Laura Berry, Megan Walker, Carol Murray, Sam Dean, Daniel Ward, Josh Ward, Toni Cartmill, Hillary Curtis, Jonathan Orr, Mandy Orr, Michael Pacheco, and Jessica Moffatt, I'm incredibly blessed to have worked alongside such an incredible group of learning all-stars.

To the rest of the FWMSH friends I have known over the last thirty-four years, please write your name here: _____. This book is dedicated to you too. Thank you for spending time with me at such a great place.

I love you all to the trepanning cavemen and back.

To the whole Gilpin crew, I love you all. Logan, thanks for making me drive that bus on video. Jenny, thanks for your constant encouragement. Rocky, thanks for being a mentor, a local historian, an author, and an all-around rad dude. Lily, thanks for helping me test labs on the bus!

To my friend Angie Kraus, for green-lighting my very first science club—your brave spirit has opened the door for tens of thousands of hours of meaningful science learning in our community. You are a wonderful educator. Keep charging forward.

To Darcy Massey, queen of after-school programs at Clayton YES! Thank you for your encouragement and support. They have provided a wonderful environment for adventures in science.

To my Science Club teammates, it is a wonderful privilege to work with such an adventurous group of science lovers! Jessie Small, Ally Crass, Lacy Crass, Brye Hutchinson, Sharron Murphree, Leslee Browning, Lisann De Weirdt, Dane Crass, and

Jackson Small, I couldn't imagine a better team to dissect diapers and explore crab guts with!

To the incredibly talented and knowledgeable science educators who make up the Metroplex Area Science Supervisors (MASS)—I'm always amazed at the depth and breadth of support that these leaders show to each other. Keep up the great work! Special thanks to Cyndy Cox for inviting me to the group.

To my ever-so-patient teammates, Katie Pogue, Erin Meyer, Jeff Lofland, and Sandy Kelsven, you guys are wonderful. Thanks for putting up with my sauerkraut and dead chicken labs. We need to get together soon.

To my Jackson, Mary, Ben, and Sarah—I never dreamed how wonderful it would be to be your dad. Thanks for helping to explore cool science!

And most of all, to my wife, Jessie—you are an incredible woman. I've never met anybody else who could manage a household of six, work multiple jobs, tolerate a sink full of crustaceans, paint a room, audit business accounts, and nurse a baby. *All at the same time.* You are amazing, and I love you the most.

Introduction

● ● ●

THANK YOU FOR PICKING UP *The Science Club Handbook*!

Why should you create a science club? Starting a science club has been the most exciting and freeing thing I have done as a teacher, and it has been the single most important change I have made to my practice. Having taught biology in third, fourth, fifth, and sixth grades and in high school, I fully appreciate the immense pressures placed on teachers. We face constantly looming threats of standardized testing and the demand that we convert students into statistics.

I'm not the only teacher tired of meetings where I assess results of a test I didn't design, in a curriculum I wasn't allowed to plan. Worse is returning to face my bored class to announce that drudgery will remain because we only have time for test prep, and then it's time for testing again. I didn't become a teacher to show my two lowest subpopulations how to choose a testing strategy. *Snooooooore.*

It's no wonder that by middle school, students say they don't like science. What they really mean is *they don't like being bored. Neither do I.* Creating a science club has let me cancel out a large number of these pressures. I get to plan labs that are interesting, no mountain of tests is tied to them, and students are thankful to be learning real stuff. By providing quality enrichment for students without taking away from instructional time, my administrators are thankful. And students have *almost* as much fun in Science Club as I do, so I am *very, very* thankful.

Science Club is now a huge lever that I use to impact instruction. My clubs meet weekly, so each member enjoys thirty-two hours of extra hands-on science every year. With twenty-five members, that's over six hundred *extra* hours of student instruction.

The principal doesn't have to fund a tutoring budget for those hours, and students beg to attend. The feedback from parents, students, and administrators is overwhelmingly positive. And on the days Science Club meetings conflict with staff meetings, administrators are always willing to send me an e-mail about what I missed.

Science clubs are a win all the way around, and this book provides a useful framework for establishing science clubs so you can enjoy a return to enjoyable education. The first six chapters provide the blueprint for building your science club, and the seventh chapter provides ten lesson plans that have been well honed by explorations of hundreds of students. I currently use the strategies and labs in this book to coordinate science clubs on multiple campuses, and as of this writing, Science Club has expanded to ten schools, with over 225 members. That equals more than seven thousand hours of student instruction every year that consistently begins with, "I can't wait to see what lab we are doing today!"

Creating a science club allows teachers and members to pursue their interests in science, and it also exposes students to the concrete experiences necessary to grow their science knowledge (or to raise their test scores if you're into that sort of thing). With this guide, you'll harness the fact that every kid is interested in a catapult, a candle, and a catfish. Hopefully not within the same lab, but to each their own...If you enjoy connecting with other science lovers, you can find me by e-mail at alan@worthlearning.org or on Twitter: @TheFort_FW. Happy exploring!

Alan Small

CHAPTER 1

Why Start a Science Club?

● ● ●

ESTABLISHING A SCIENCE CLUB PROVIDES huge benefits for your learning community, and the benefits do not just belong to the students! Teachers, administrators, parents, and even school budgets benefit from the program.

INCREASED INSTRUCTIONAL TIME

Students who join Science Club instantly have increased instructional time over nonmembers simply by virtue of adding an hour of Science Club each week. I begin my clubs several weeks after the start of school and end them the week before school releases for summer. This means I will have thirty-two hour-long meetings during the school year. If each student normally receives an hour of regular science instruction each day (we can all dream, can't we?), then a school year should give each student 180 hours of science instruction. A student who joins Science Club has 17.7 percent more instruction than nonmembers. And teachers near and far will acknowledge that *180 hours is a best-case scenario that rarely happens.* The reality is that most schools will have an increase of 25–30 percent or even 50 percent in instructional time for members. Unless, of course, you have the situation where science is disregarded or postponed until after the standardized tests. In that case, Science Club may be the only science instruction some students are getting (heaven forbid).

AUTHENTIC EXPERIENCES

Students need to *touch* science. Hearing about it is fine, and reading about it is OK too. Even watching a video about science has value. But if you want your kids to enjoy science, they have to *experience* it themselves. They need to put their hands into science, they need to lay their cheeks on the table and watch science, they need to rub science on their taste buds, and they need to push the launch button and smell the science. Real-life, concrete experiences are what stick in the mind, and they are the types of learning students will hook future learning onto. Science Club pours these experiences directly into the brains of every member, and that is a very comforting thought at the end of the year.

There is no need to color pumpkin pictures
when you are a dissection expert!

STRONGER STUDENT RELATIONSHIPS

Students, teachers, and everybody on Earth build relationships with the people they spend time with. The more we talk and share with each other, the stronger our relationships are. We learn what the people around us like, what energizes them, and what their sensitivities are. *And hopefully we make friends.* The trouble in the regular classroom is that pressure is on to keep the curriculum and instruction flowing hard and fast during every available minute. Staff meetings are filled with reminders that "We teach from bell to bell on this campus." My teacher appraisal has a section showing how many students are "on task" when my administrator breezes through. One year I even had a principal insist that all teachers carry instructional materials in the halls so the walk to lunch and the line outside PE would still be productive learning time. With pressure like that, there isn't time for finding out how Jackson's weekend was or what Mary saw at the lake yesterday. There definitely isn't time to let everybody talk about the crystal that Ben found on vacation.

This high flow of instruction can easily squash opportunities for students to get to know each other. Students spend seven hours a day together, but relationship time is squeezed into the thirty-minute lunch time (if they aren't sitting silently), during the ten-minute recess (if your school even has recess), or after school (if two kids happen to live close to each other). Is it any wonder that students don't know how to treat each other or that they sneak into the bathroom to visit? I have had fifth graders not know the names of classmates they have shared a room with all year long. I've had students in the class next door pass me in the hall every day, and I couldn't tell you their names, much less their hobbies or what they like and dislike. That is embarrassing and maddening.

A Great Antidote for Missing Social Times

Students get to sit with friends and share their latest addition to the feather collection or discuss the changing colors of leaves in the fall. I also get to spend time watching what noises make the kids giggle in the sound lab and which students will turn green when they see bugs. We all get to know each other, and the nicest part is that these relationships bridge across classrooms and grade levels. It's common to see second graders and fourth graders pair up in a way that just isn't possible during the regular school day. It gives me a warm, fuzzy feeling each time I see Science Club members waving to each other across the lunchroom or down the hall. I never have to deal with bullying issues in Science Club because the students know each other well enough to not use those behaviors as a crutch. Over time, members of Science Club accumulate more time together in shared, meaningful learning than my regular students spend at recess in the entire year.

Easy Classroom Management

If I haven't gotten the point across yet, let me point out that science clubs are a very specialized group of learners who are much gentler on a teacher's psyche than a normal classroom. Behavioral and social challenges that must be managed during the day just seem to evaporate once the science-club meeting begins. Besides the high-interest content and the strong relationships that are built within the club, there is the difference that Science Club is a *self-selecting group*. Students are not required to join, but rather they *choose* to join. *Beg* may even be a better word. The students who end up being members have chosen to be there, and they are already mentally primed for action. There are usually several avid science enthusiasts within the group, and the success of each lab is greater with each meeting due to their enthusiasm. This happy progress converts more students to enthusiastic science lovers, leading to an ever-improving cycle of science awesomeness. Science Club has become a happy, stress-free home for the following folks:

- Kids who are too fidgety or dyslexic to spend time reading science texts
- The boy who is diagnosed as being on the autism spectrum and has a physics obsession
- The girl who has trouble connecting socially
- The gifted and talented student who constantly misbehaves out of boredom
- The kids who keep getting suspended for bullying and fighting on the playground
- The average student who relishes any chance to become an expert in something

Science Club students are as diverse and interesting as my normal classroom students, but somehow they never have time to get off task or misbehave. I have never had to remove a student from Science Club for behavior. Actually, the opposite is true. The office knows to check Science Club first if there is a missing student after school, because students have been known to sneak out of the bus line at dismissal just to attend a meeting.

On a side note, it's possible to have science clubs that are not self-selected. I've been on campuses requiring after-school tutoring for struggling students. It's possible that students could be selected to attend Science Club because of grades, and they aren't primed for science learning on the first day. Don't let that throw you off your game. When that happens, just call the tutoring "Science Club," and carry on. Students will join the cycle of science awesomeness after a meeting or two.

BUILDING TWENTY-FIRST-CENTURY SKILLS

According to the Partnership for 21st Century Learning mastery of key subjects and twenty-first-century themes is essential to student success.[1] Science falls *squarely* into the key-subjects category. Creativity and innovation, critical thinking and problem solving, and communication and collaboration skills are all included in the skills that students should cultivate to succeed in life. A science club is a natural fit for learning these skills and is by far the easiest place for me to teach them. For example, it is common in a science club to have members working in small groups to design and test solutions to engineering problems and then share results with the group. The students are usually too busy playing with their bridges and roller coasters to notice their improved communication and critical thinking skills, but what they don't know won't hurt them.

JOYFUL LEARNING

If anybody asks what makes a science club great, I can explain the academic and social benefits of starting a club. There are so many great things about science clubs that presenting or defending the idea to administrators is easy. But I rarely present my main motivation for starting science clubs, because it isn't measurable, and it isn't part of the standards. It may even be self-indulgent. My main motivation is that *I enjoy Science Club*, and so do my students.

To the number crunchers and policy wonks, that may seem frivolous. I don't really care. They don't know what I know. They don't know that learning happens best when we enjoy ourselves. In nearly every instance, we learn what we play with, and we play

---

1 Cator et. al., Framework for 21st Century Learning, 1)

with the things we enjoy. Take a moment and think of something you are good at. Anything—swimming, cooking, skateboarding, gardening, singing, video games, or whatever. If you are good at that subject, I'm sure you have spent a good chunk of time playing around with it. If you have played around with it, it is undoubtedly because you enjoyed it.

In Science Club, creating enjoyment is my secret mission. If the enjoyment happens, all the other benefits happen automagically. My favorite sound is hearing a group of students cheer when a challenging activity is successful. My favorite sight is watching students' mouths fly open in wonder when they watch their rocket fly, or they see the acids magically change color. They can't wait to drag their friends over to show what they've done, and their parents always get an earful at pickup time. If I can enjoy my work, it might be worth doing. If kids have half as much fun as I do, they will be having a ball.

CHAPTER 2

Getting Started

● ● ●

IN THIS SECTION, YOU'LL LEARN answers to these important questions:

- Who gets invited to Science Club?
- How do you plan meetings?
- How do you get students, parents, and administrators to fall in love with Science Club?

And most importantly,

- Who is going to pay for all this?

Inviting the Right Kids

Who should you invite to join Science Club? Science Club is your party, so you should be able to invite who you want to. Still, you ought to be intentional about who you want to join so you can enjoy the most benefit from your meetings. There is a good chance that administrator approval will hinge on which set of students you plan to invite. Below are several different groups I have invited to Science Club. Each of these groups worked fine, but they each had their own unique feel during the meetings. Copy one of the formats below, or craft a plan that sounds perfect to you. Just make sure to set up a group that you want to be with during meetings. Feel free to be creative when planning your group. I've experimented with a wide variety of scientists, and you can too. (I've even had a science club of homeschooled teens who wanted to learn science while socializing with friends.)

I've started clubs with the following age groups:

* Only third, fourth, and fifth graders invited
* All grades on campus invited (kindergarten through fourth graders)
* All grades on campus invited (fifth and sixth graders)
* Only fifth graders needing tutoring help invited

Only Third, Fourth, and Fifth Graders Invited

My very first science club was on a kindergarten through fifth-grade campus. I set up a science club that invited third-, fourth-, and fifth-grade students to join. I had previously taught each of those grades, and I knew I would survive working with those students.

The original plan was to meet after school, once a week on Tuesdays for *eight weeks*, and there would be twenty-five spots available. I made an overhead announcement and asked the third-, fourth-, and fifth-grade teachers to pass invitations out at the end of the day.

The next morning when I got to school, I was stunned to find a line of students outside my door ready to hand in their registration sheets. By the time morning announcements were over twenty minutes later, *every slot was full*, and I had several kids on a waiting list. My principal quickly agreed to let me open a second section to meet on Thursdays, and it filled the following day.

That semester, fifty students enjoyed fermenting sauerkraut, playing with slime, and dissecting catfish. I fell in love with Science Club. The feedback was great, and the younger students who were not participating would often come up and ask if Science Club would meet again the following year so they could join.

ALL GRADES ON CAMPUS INVITED (KINDERGARTEN THROUGH FOURTH GRADERS)

My second version of science club was on a kindergarten through fourth-grade campus. I opened up registration to every grade level, and we planned to meet once a week after school on Tuesdays for the entire semester. The twenty-five spots filled faster than I could keep track of, so I actually ended up with thirty kids across all grade levels.

I initially worried the younger students might hold the labs back. I *did* end up tying more sneakers and handing out more tissues than usual, but the unflagging curiosity and amped-up enthusiasm of the younger students more than made up for any required mucus maintenance. We all packed into the Science Lab, and we designed towers, dissected crayfish, and experimented with acids and bases.

ALL GRADES ON CAMPUS INVITED (FIFTH AND SIXTH GRADERS)

My third version of science club was a bit different because it was held at a fifth- and sixth-grade intermediate school. We also met once a week for the entire semester. The campus was a feeder school for several local elementary schools. It was much larger than my previous campuses, but somehow the larger school didn't translate to a larger science club. Instead of filling all twenty-five slots, membership topped out at fourteen kids. I could tell students of this age had to choose between a much larger set of after-school activities than students at the elementary level. Some students who would have joined previously were now playing soccer, joining theater, or were old enough to ride the bus home and stay by themselves until their parents got home.

I worried that the smaller membership would hurt the club, but *I was wrong*. Meetings seemed to always go deeper into the content than I expected. There were more thoughtful questions and "happy discoveries" than usual, and the background knowledge that kids brought with them was obviously deeper than most elementary students. On more than one occasion, a member would jump up from his or her lab and run to grab a tablet or phone out of a backpack to show his or her partners a video related to the topic of the day. These students were more likely to continue labs at home or initiate new labs independently on their own time and then bring them to Science Club to show off to their friends. We built rockets, hunted fossils, and designed xylophones.

And the next semester, we filled twenty-nine out of twenty-five slots for Science Club. I guess some of the theater kids changed their minds.

ONLY FIFTH GRADERS NEEDING TUTORING HELP INVITED
Version number four of science club was a different animal altogether. A friend of mine at a local elementary school was looking for ways to boost science scores for fifth-grade students. Fifth grade is when local students take state standardized science tests, so pressure was on to raise student performance. The campus had prekindergarten through fifth-grade students, but we only invited *fifth-grade students* so that there would be a larger benefit for that year's scores.

Students on this campus were (unfortunately) accustomed to receiving "invitations" to after-school tutoring sessions, which are usually similar to regular school-day activities. The science instructional coach e-mailed me some testing strategies to work on and a few practice test questions to go over for good measure. It really wasn't any surprise when the invitations went out and only four students joined. No doubt their parents forced them.

For the first lab, I made sure to bring in a physics activity that students *always* get excited about—we built marble roller coasters out of swimming-pool noodles. It is a loud, colorful event that always spills into the hallway or rolls out across the cafeteria. Halfway through the first meeting, I passed out M&Ms to the eager engineers, and I somehow conveniently forgot to mention the practice test questions.

By the third meeting, we had ten members. We dissected the smelliest crayfish I could find, and within a month, there were twenty-five members. We never picked up a pencil, the kids enjoyed themselves so much they were sad when the club ended, and the principal offered me a classroom teaching job for the upcoming school year. It was wildly successful, and we immediately began planning for the following school year.

Hopefully seeing the variation in the grade levels will encourage you to set up a club that works perfectly for you. I haven't found an age group yet that dislikes Science Club. Different income levels haven't affected membership, either. The above examples are pretty evenly split between low-income Title I campuses and well-to-do campuses where every student carries around his or her own tablet and cell phone. Across the board, *students want to have fun learning science.*

On a side note, I plan science clubs to be on campus during the school year because it fits my schedule. Clubs could also be held over the summer, in community centers and libraries, at museums and science centers, or with a dedicated group of homeschool students. The science-club model is flexible enough that you can adapt it to whatever situation you like.

GETTING APPROVED TO START A CLUB

Implementing and maintaining a club will be your responsibility and ultimately your claim to fame as a campus science rock star. You will be the administrator of your own group of science enthusiasts! But before you send out fliers, you need to make sure your plan is known and accepted by the campus administrator (usually the principal) who is in charge of your school. If he or she is on board, it'll make your year much smoother. It's time to start thinking like an administrator to figure out how to get approved.

School administrators are swamped daily with decisions. They have to make multiple tricky decisions about every facet of the school, every hour of the day. Do you remember that student they helped you with last week? Your principal has one of those kids in *every class*—with a parent to contact. And the copy machine is broken. And the curriculum coordinator needs to meet. And the playground monitor just called in sick. And...and...and...

So what is the best way to get administrator support? *Propose instead of ask!*

Every decision takes up computing space in their brain. Principals need to find useful conclusions to each decision quickly, or they'll get buried with unsolved problems. Administrators can't afford to make decisions that generate ten new decisions, and they don't have time to approve something that will force them to work harder later. *The less your principal has to think about the idea, the greater the chances of approval.*

Don't expect them to plan the details for you! When it's time to propose your science club, pitch the proposal that *you* would like to have. Every detail that you ask the principal to come up with moves your approval a little closer to the "Let me think about it, and I'll get back to you" pile.

Instead of asking:	Propose the following:
Who should I invite?	I'd like to invite fourth and fifth graders.
What should we learn about?	We'll be learning in fun labs that support standards.
What day would you let us meet?	I'd like to meet Mondays after school.
Is there a space I can use?	Meetings can be in my room or the cafeteria.

If you have your proposal already in mind, you can present a choice that is a simple yes/no request for your principal. If they say yes, you are good to go. If they say no, it will probably be because something on campus conflicts with part of your proposal, and you can make adjustments to your plan for a better fit. For example, choir may meet Mondays after school, so it would keep some students from joining Science Club. If you adjust your time to a different day, the problem is solved. To present your idea, you'll need to iron out your five *W*s and present them as a proposal.

* *Who* will be invited to your science club, and who will manage it?
* *What* will be your goals?
* *When* will meetings be?
* *Where* will the meetings be?
* *Why* is a science club a good fit for your campus?

Try your best to find a time when your principal is not swamped by meetings and parent conferences, and stop by *in person* to make your proposal, if at all possible. Depending on how accessible your principal is, you may need to make an appointment to meet, but making proposals in person greatly increases your odds of getting approved. It's easier to deny an e-mailed request, because e-mails are impersonal. Asking in person personalizes the request and makes the concept more concrete in your principal's mind. Also, there may be pieces of information missing from your proposal that he or she needs for approval. If you are there in person, you can provide that information on the spot. If you have just thrown your proposal into an e-mail, they may have to deny the request just to streamline their daily decision list instead of taking fifteen minutes to compose an e-mail back to you.

It will take a little back-and-forth to get the details honed and polished with the principal, but that negotiation and discussion is a great process for ensuring a science club is a good fit not only for you but for the whole campus.

Choosing a Meeting Location

Meetings can be held anywhere there is room. I have held meetings in the following places:

- My classroom
- Another teacher's classroom
- The cafeteria
- The library
- The science lab
- The teacher's lounge
- A hallway
- The gym
- The playground
- The little grass yard next to the parking lot

Don't worry about whether or not the meeting itself can be held in a certain space. Nearly every space is suitable for holding the actual meeting—your kids would meet on the roof if you would let them! *What you need is a space that allows easy setup and cleanup and integration into the campus schedule.*

Setup

Is the space available for a reasonable setup at the beginning of the meeting? The transition from normal school day to Science Club happens quickly, so the easier the setup, the better. When members dismiss from class and line up outside the meeting area, I have noticed that the faster I can lay out the supplies and invite them in, the easier the meeting. The longer students wait in the hall, the more wound up they get; especially since they have been sitting in class for the last seven hours.

If you are a teacher, the easiest place to set up is probably your classroom because you know where everything is, and you can have things laid out in advance of the meeting. There is also the comfort of being in your own space. There may be times, though, where your room is not a good choice. Maybe it's needed for a tutoring space, or the heat and air conditioning is turned off when school dismisses. In some cases, the number of students in Science Club won't fit comfortably into a classroom. Maybe you don't even have your own classroom!

Don't let any of that stop you. You just need a way to get to your meeting area. In the years where I needed to move rooms, I kept a rolling cart in my classroom, and I prepped everything for Science Club there (or I asked the first two Science Club members who arrived to help me with the task). Students would meet at my door, and I would walk the line to the cafeteria or the library, and

Lunchrooms work great
for large activities!

we would hold meetings using the supplies that were on my cart. If you can't find a cart, just ask the students to help carry supplies. They love to help, and they'll be eager to help get the meeting started.

Cleanup

How easy will cleanup be at the end of the lab? Having a sink close by is nice when you need to wash hands and rinse brushes! And nothing beats the convenience of the rolling trash cans they have in the cafeteria. If you don't have one of your own in your classroom, I highly recommend borrowing one. Cleanup becomes a breeze.

In a perfect world, meetings will end in enough time to have students clean up. But if you are like me, sometimes you'll lose track of time, and you'll have to line everyone up quickly for dismissal without getting the room cleaned back to 100 percent. In that case, it falls to you to clean things, and some spaces are easier than others to clean! Dumping forty glasses of colored water is easy if you have a sink nearby. If you have to carry them all down the hall to the bathroom, you might as well put your headphones on to enjoy the workout. Sweeping glitter and sand off a tile floor takes about sixty seconds, but if you have to hunt for a vacuum cleaner for carpet in the library, you aren't going home anytime soon.

When you end up with a messy room, remember that twenty kids cleaning for thirty seconds is the same as you cleaning alone for ten minutes.

Pro tip: If there are any teachers' kids who are members, there is a chance they'll hang around a little to help. If you frame it right, they'll think it's better than sitting in their moms' or dads' rooms staring at the wall or doing homework.

Fitting into the Campus Schedule

Think about if a space is available when you need it. Is there any other group or activity that might conflict with the time that you will meet? What meetings, tutoring groups, childcare providers, and other clubs meet after school? Plan for a space that coexists easily with them.

The cafeteria has always been a great meeting space for me, but then again, it is a great meeting space for everybody. Special events like the science fair, PTA meetings, and Meet the Teacher nights are often using that space, too. Luckily, special events are usually held in the evenings, so they don't often conflict with Science Club times.

Remember that a little flexibility will do wonders for your stress level. (Surprise! The pest-control guy is here to spray your room!) When your meeting location gets a sudden change, just go with it. Schools are fluid and unpredictable places, and it won't do you any good to stomp your foot. If you are flexible enough to make adjustments as needed, your science club will be a huge success, and your coworkers will come to know you as a dependable partner who is focused on creating a successful learning environment for students.

And you will get to have the science club again next year.

Set a Meeting Time

Choosing a meeting time for your science club is an easier decision than deciding the location. All you need to nail down is the day of the week and the time meetings will be held. I have settled on meeting *once a week, after school, for one hour.*

Once a Week

Meetings that are held once a week give members something to look forward to, and they are consistent enough to develop routines, but they are spaced out enough to prevent kids from getting bored or me getting overwhelmed with planning. I have held meetings on each of the weekdays and have never had trouble with any of them. The significant things to consider when choosing a day is when other clubs meet and when staff meetings occur.

Pro tip: If you are sick of staff meetings that suck your soul, plan your meetings to conflict with them. (Sorry, ma'am, I have twenty kids elbow deep in a pumpkin dissection right now. You know how it is. Can you record it for me? Thanks!)

After School

After school is by far the easiest time to hold meetings. Parents don't need to drop off their child because he or she is already at school. It doesn't require extra effort to pick up at 4:00 p.m. instead of 3:00 p.m., and they get to avoid the normal dismissal crowd of parents. After-school meetings also relieve the pressure of curriculum requirements, and you won't lose classroom instructional time like you would if you held meetings during the school day. *See below for a case study on a principal who failed to implement clubs during the school day.*

One down side to holding meetings after school is that students who depend on the bus to get home might not be able to join. Without alternative transportation, the science club might be out of reach for them.

Holding meetings before school has never fit my morning routines, but it would be possible, and it might be a useful strategy for including the bus-riding kids. The buses usually get to school in time for breakfast, so students might be present in time to hold a short meeting if they were allowed to eat breakfast during the lab.

On a side note, energy levels may start to drop by midafternoon, since lunch is a distant memory. Consider letting kids bring a snack to meetings to help keep their energy levels up.

FOR ONE HOUR

An hour allows time for student arrival, for me to explain a lab, let the students complete the lab, and then clean up, but an hour is *not* so long that students get tired or bored. An hour is easy for parents and other teachers to remember, and it probably won't increase the time you spend on campus. Hour-long meetings also allow you to mirror after-school tutoring sessions that are held for the hour after school is out. Limiting meetings to an hour also avoids scheduling conflicts with evening events like soccer practice, scout meetings, and church services.

I have experimented with meetings that lasted up to three hours, and there are some nice things about long-format meetings. Students are not pressed for time to complete labs, and they have deeper experience with the content. We also enjoy more comprehensive discussions about what we are exploring, and I am more likely to join in with experiments and discussions, which is a nice break from the role of instructor.

Unfortunately, downsides of longer meetings have been more severe than upsides. Longer meetings require longer workdays for me. They require more content and materials, so my workload and budget increase. Fewer students are available for longer meetings, so membership will shrink, which narrows the impact and benefits of your science club. Also, students get tired and hungry in longer meetings, so I spend more time managing conflict. Ultimately, longer meetings were better than no meetings, but not as good as a single hour.

Case Study: The Clubs That Ate a Principal

A new elementary school principal decided to make a few changes on campus. During a staff meeting, it was announced that every teacher would be required to create and sponsor a club. Once a week, all clubs would meet for one hour *during the school day,* and students would get to decide which club they should join. To create a "fun environment," the principal left themes, strategies, and projects to the teachers to come up with. Teachers could plan clubs however they wanted, as long as students had *lots of fun.* Messes should be allowed, entertainment should be high, and that was that.

Nobody trained the teachers how to provide meaningful learning outside of normal instruction. Nobody pointed out that successful clubs are more than messy activities and loud students. Nobody planned a framework for how students should approach this new type of learning. Without any substantial plan to work with, teacher buy-in for the clubs remained low.

Each week during club hour, there would be a whole campus of kids milling about, trying to decide whether they liked chess, cooking, or robotics. Students who had been trained in their classrooms to learn only the correct answers were frustrated by the open-ended nature of many of the clubs. They chased their friends from club to club, rarely staying long enough to have meaningful experiences.

Standing in each classroom was a bewildered teacher struggling to plan a club meeting while still providing normal classroom instruction. They had spent years collecting and honing strategies for their regular classes, and now those strategies didn't apply. They didn't want to get in trouble for not planning a club the right way, but they didn't want to look stupid for having to ask how to set one up. Teachers ultimately felt ungrounded and helpless when pressed into holding clubs without training and support on how to hold meetings.

Over time, the principal became irate because nobody was "doing it right." Visiting different club meetings provided a chance to micromanage and redirect students and teachers, but the input was never well received. The normal e-mail directives and classroom observations didn't work. Staff meetings, consultants, crowd funding campaigns, and website pictures didn't help either. The entire school was sinking into a hole that was just getting deeper. Most of the teaching staff turned over the following year, but that did very little to perk up the campus atmosphere. Clubs with low numbers of students were looked down on, and clubs with high numbers became stressful and unproductive. Stress, jealousy, and fear began breaking down staff relationships, and the regular classroom instruction quickly suffered. With such a profound downhill slide, the principal was abruptly reassigned in the middle of the year. A new principal came in to revive the campus, and of course, clubs were eliminated in the process.

The takeaway. The principal had hoped by declaring clubs into existence, the school would end up full of excited students and teachers milling about in the ecstasy of learning. Unfortunately for the principal, *creating a new environment is more complicated than just making declarations.* To be successful with such an ambitious plan, a strong leader needs to *guide* the entire process with a large amount of teacher training, input, and planning. Students need a system for choosing a club, and each club needs a clear set of objectives to work toward. These need to happen well in advance of starting the program. With this support in place, teachers can enjoy the confidence to commit fully to their club, and the principal can turn control over to the individual clubs.

Funding Science Club: Who Is Going to Pay for All This?

Club materials don't have to be expensive or even cost anything at all, but having a supply budget increases learning and enjoyment faster than just scraping by. A budget also eases planning pressures on the instructor. When I have had little time to prepare, buying interesting supplies has helped me keep student-interest levels high.

Example. Today you have a science-club meeting after school, but you haven't had time to plan the meeting. You *could* skip your conference and lunch period to put together a plan, but yuck. Instead, stop at the store on the way to school and pick up ten dollars' worth of fishing worms and a bag of gummy-worm candy. With your live specimens ready to go and your edible samples ready to pass out, you have an instant meeting! You can do the same thing with whole shrimp, balloons and straws, paper airplanes, baking soda and vinegar, mealworms, dry ice, and goldfish, for instance.

At the time of this writing, I budget one dollar per child on supplies for each meeting. With twenty-five students, that's about the cost of dinner for two at a dine-in restaurant, and it's an amount that provides really rich experiences within meetings. Labs can be conducted for *significantly* less, but it's nice to play with a good collection of materials.

Below is a set of strategies to help fund your science club. Each has its own benefits. If spending money gives you stress, skip to the end for ways to reduce or even eliminate supply costs.

Teacher Funded

Buying materials out of your own pocket lets you immediately begin purchasing supplies without coordinating with other people or dealing with budgeting and accounting. It's your money; spend it how you like. Teacher-funded clubs also enjoy the flexibility to change plans quickly without advanced planning.

The downside of paying for materials yourself is that you alone shoulder the financial burden, but most meetings can be supplied without breaking the bank. The upside is your purchases are yours to keep forever, even if you switch schools.

PTA/PTO Funded

If your campus has a Parent-Teacher Association/Organization, you can ask for help with purchasing supplies. PTAs are usually set up as nonprofit organizations, which means that when they make money (remember all those fundraisers?), they aren't doing it to get rich. To keep the IRS from getting grumpy, the money that is accumulated *must get spent!* Happy day for you!

Approach a PTA board member and ask him or her about funding supplies for your science club. Don't let the title *board member* scare you. Board members are just teachers who offer to help out or parents who have time to assist the school. Chances are if you are the type to start a science club, you are already on the board yourself, or you will be soon. After you let the board know the benefits of a science club, the topic can be discussed at the next board meeting, and members will vote on whether or not to spend the money.

There are a couple of challenges with using PTA money. You have to do some advance planning by gathering a list of supply costs so PTA has an amount to vote on. It's easiest if the supplies come from one place, so PTA just makes one large purchase. I like to use Amazon.com or a science-supply company. Also, the timing is kind of slow—you have to wait for the next board meeting, which can add several weeks to your process, and if you order supplies online, you have to wait for delivery.

One challenge unique for many PTAs is the requirement in their bylaws that money spent from their budget must benefit *all students* on campus. This prevents one parent or teacher from putting pressure on the board to spend the entire budget on a single classroom. A solution to the "whole campus" requirement is to open registration up to all students on campus. You will still close registration when the club is full, but everybody had an equal chance to register. Also, I have offered to host campus Family Science nights using the purchased materials to extend the reach to the whole campus.

The process is more complicated than teacher-funded clubs, but you can get quite a bit of money toward your club with the PTA's help. Because the PTA benefits the whole school, they are accustomed to spending hundreds or thousands of dollars at a time.

Pro tip: When the PTA buys a ton of cool science gadgetry for a science club, don't forget to use those goodies in your classroom! If you share with your fellow teachers, they will love you forever.

STUDENT FUNDED

This is how I fund meetings now, and it works regardless of the poverty/affluence level of the campus. Students bring supply money, and I spend it on supplies. If each member contributes a single dollar per meeting, there is plenty of money for materials. (These dollar amounts are from 2016. The farther into the future you are, the more you'll need to adjust the dollar amounts.)

Parents like spending money for Science Club. No matter their situation, Science Club presents a great value. If they want their child to be a super smart scientist someday, Science Club is the perfect solution. If they worry about idle hands while they are at work, Science Club keeps kids busy. If they can't stand their own child, then a dollar for an hour away from junior is the best deal in town. Whatever the case, I want kids in Science Club, and parents are happy to accommodate.

On campuses in middle- or upper-income levels, it's simplest to have kids register for the year at a dollar per meeting. If Science Club meets weekly for the year, registration is around thirty-five dollars. That amount will be easy enough for most families, and if they pay all at once, you only have registrations once a year.

For campuses at lower-income levels, divide the year into smaller sections. Instead of the whole year, have members register for a semester or for a shorter time period. If members register for two months for eight dollars, nearly every family could come up with that amount. If that still seems unreasonable, go for one month.

Caution: Before you ask for money, consider that mishandling funds is the easiest way around to *lose your job*. Just imagine the following headline in the local newspaper:

TEACHER CHARGES STUDENTS TO "JOIN HER SPECIAL CLUB!"

Stranger things have happened.

You need *very clear communication* with your administrators about what your money plan is and how to keep track of cash handling. It's unlikely your school wants you to keep $900 in cash in your desk drawer, so learn your campus procedures. Maybe money gets locked in the office safe until you turn in receipts. Maybe it gets deposited into your school's bank account, and you get reimbursed. It's possible the money goes straight to the campus secretary to get deposited, and you don't even touch it. It will be up to you to understand campus procedures.

If the school has no rules for cash handling, *watch out!* You are on your own to protect yourself from any impression that money *could* be misspent. Keep every receipt for every purchase, and be ready to show them to parents, principals, newspaper reporters, and the IRS when the time comes. Don't buy coffee with it, or "borrow" from it like the church secretary and the little league coach you read about in the news every few weeks.

How should you collect supply fees? If members submit a supply fee, remember *cash is king.* Cash doesn't bounce, get canceled, or end up copied by a hacker. Checks are a bad idea because you have to run them through your personal bank account (just don't), or you deposit them with the school and then fight to get access to the money after they clear. In a group the size of a science club, you'll have a bad check or two, and then you have to call parents and talk about insufficient funds—yuck. Running credit cards is beyond the time commitment of overworked teachers, and the chance of losing control of somebody's financial information is too risky. *Cash is the way to go.*

Grant Funded

The largest source of money available for teachers is also the most ignored. Grants give teachers funding for innovative projects and programs to expand their educational reach. Grants are the education world's version of writing a business plan to attract investors. There are so many places to get grant money that entire businesses exist just to accumulate lists of available grants!

Two challenges prevent teachers from going after the big money:

* Teachers don't have experience with grant writing.
* Teachers have an unwillingness to commit time to something that might not work out.

The first challenge is remedied with a simple solution: *complete a grant application, and click* **send**. After that, you are a grant writer! You have more experience applying for grants than 90 percent of teachers out there! It doesn't matter if you get the first grant or not—you are still a grant writer.

The second challenge is more philosophical. It's reasonable to avoid wasting time on tasks with no benefit, but the rewards of grant writing are large enough that you can strike out a few times and still end up with a good return for your efforts. Imagine spending three hours writing a grant for $500, and then you get denied. Then the same thing happens again. And then again. But then on the fourth try, the grant gets awarded. That would be a total of twelve hours of work for $500. That divides out to over forty dollars an hour. Not bad for money you plucked from the air!

Two encouraging thoughts:

* I have never seen anyone get denied three times in a row. Organizations that make grant money available *want you to have the money*!
* I have never seen anybody write a grant for such a small amount. Most small classroom grants I have encountered have been in the $1,000 to $5,000 range. If you spent twelve

hours on a $5,000 grant, your efforts would generate over $400 per hour! I have managed education grants of over $900,000, and I can tell you that using grant money to fund cool teaching projects is a great way to go!

If you love the idea of using grant money to rev up your instruction, you can search for education grants in your area and then start submitting applications.

Reducing Costs or Forget Funding Altogether

Sometimes a budget makes things too complicated. A lack of time, staff, or support might mean there isn't a way to manage any money. *Don't let that stop you.* Here are several strategies to have great meetings with little or no money:

Science Supply Closet

Most schools have a storage area for science supplies. Go through that pile, and pull out the cool stuff to use (like the dusty old stream table nobody has touched in ten years). If you find a piece of equipment you don't recognize, just Google it. Or better yet, search for it on YouTube. Somebody out there has posted a video of it, and in two minutes, you'll be an expert.

Donated Stuff

A vast ocean of supplies is waiting for you at your students' homes and in other classrooms. Besides normal school supplies, things like soda bottles, yarn, sugar, baking soda, rocks, cardboard, and hand mirrors are all available to you. You just need to ask for them. Here's how:

* Ask members to bring supplies that you need.
* Post a Wanted sign at your door that has a list of needed things.
* E-mail the campus and ask, "Does anybody have extra ___ that I can have?"
* Ask teachers to save their soda bottles after their holiday parties.
* Use your newsletter and/or website to ask for needed supplies.
* Connect parents to a texting service at the beginning of the year, and *safely* request supplies via text message. (Remind.com is great for this, and *everybody* texts.)

Outdoor Explorations

Take meetings outside for observations, explorations, and experiments using the playground equipment. It doesn't matter if the campus is surrounded with inner-city pavement or with backwoods wilderness. Biologists have studied all those things, and you can, too. *What matters is that there are questions to investigate and that you help students find an interest in the investigations.* If that isn't in your comfort level yet, get online and look up the TED Talk video by Sugata Mitra titled "The Child-Driven Education."[2] I promise it will be worth your time. His experiments show unschooled children in the slums of India learning biotechnology in a foreign

---

2 Sugata Mitra, "The Child-Driven Education" www.TED.com)

language *on their own*. Best of all, the simple strategies that he uses are a perfect fit for a science club.

TAKE-APART LAB

Using hand tools to take apart broken or old toys, appliances, and electronics is a great way to explore numerous concepts. Kids in a take-apart lab can learn about simple machines, magnets, motors, circuitry, engineering, and recycling. If you have hand tools to take things apart, use them. If not, have students bring them. Ask for donated items, or you can accumulate them yourself over time. One great trick for gathering take-apart items is to visit a thrift store and ask for the broken things they can't sell. Unusable donations arrive every day, and they usually land in a trash barrel. I have stocked many take-apart labs for free by visiting with a thrift-store manager.

Pro tip: Stay alive. Microwaves have a huge capacitor that can kill you. Old-style televisions (pre-flat-screen) are made largely of a glass tube that can explode. Printer cartridges should be removed before the kids use them for face paint.

Conducting a Take-apart lab is a great way to
explore simple machines on the cheap!

Pair Up

The supplies needed for a lab is cut in half when you pair students up. This works great for engineering challenges, dissections, and investigations. Some situations work with groups of three or even four. When we dissected an octopus, it was too expensive for each student to have one, but by forming groups of three, the supplies fit the budget with no problem. Pairing kids up increases engagement too; every time a student starts to lose focus, his or her partner helps pull the student back to the activity.

Get Trashy

Use trash, recyclables, and observation labs to explore waste streams at your school. Lunchroom waste is a great resource for composting, decomposition, worm farming, and gardening. Also, holiday parties, and the cleanup at the end of the school year have both been particularly useful for collecting school supplies, bottles, and the unwanted teaching materials from the teacher down the hall who is leaving to go to law school.

Purchase Non-consumables

Cool science toys like hand-crank generators, circuitry sets, air-rocket kits, and magnets have higher costs at the beginning, but once you have them, you can use them forever. It's worth the investment to add things like this to your science club's collection because after they are purchased, they are available for future labs for free. Don't forget they are available to use during the regular school day too!

CHASE THE HOLIDAYS
After each holiday, the price of themed merchandise that didn't sell will be greatly reduced at local stores. Easter eggs that I bought for 90 percent off turned into rocket parts, musical instruments, buoyancy tools, and projectiles. The Christmas tree stands that I found for seventy-five cents each have become my all-time favorite water tanks because they don't spill. Does it matter that the balloons and pencils have last year's Happy New Year's message? Not really. Take advantage of the markdowns to stock up on your supplies.

LEVERAGE OTHER SCIENCE LOVERS
Often you can borrow kits from museums, zoos, libraries, and community centers. Many informal education centers offer collections or thematic kits teachers can borrow for free or with a token deposit. They are often filled with specimens and artifacts curated specifically for teachers to use in their classrooms. Some museums will even assemble a collection for you based on which topic you are studying. Some even come with curriculum and activity ideas to make your life even easier.

CHAPTER 3

Recruitment: If You Build It, Will They Come?

● ● ●

How often does a teacher get to handpick their students? If you are thoughtful in recruitment, you will end up with a science-club dream team that you love. If you don't plan well, at best, your group will be a random selection of students. At worst, you'll end up with students who aren't a good fit for your science club. *Recruit thoughtfully.* I have used the following strategies to help me recruit just the right mix of science lovers for my clubs.

How Many Members?

To begin recruiting members, decide how large your club should be. The higher the number of students, the higher the cost, and the size is up to you.

I've had science clubs as small as eight students. It was nice to really get to know each student well, but when somebody was absent, it really affected the participation in the activities. On the other end of the spectrum, I've had clubs as large as forty. They are wildly popular, but you have to recruit other teachers to assist.

There seems to be a sweet spot between the minimum of fourteen members to a maximum of twenty-five. Having at least fourteen creates a certain momentum in the labs and legitimizes the time that you invest in the club. Limiting membership to twenty-five students keeps things manageable if you are working alone, and it will allow the club to fit into a regular classroom. Also, if a few students move away or join soccer during the year, Science Club will still have enough members to avoid opening registration again.

With older students, twenty-five kids still makes a nice size, but the opportunity opens to allow smaller clubs too. Smaller clubs become a little easier because students are more independent. This lets the teacher focus more on the activities and less on classroom management. It also allows one lab topic to extend beyond a single meeting, and the students who join clubs in older grades generally don't need the social velocity of a large group to keep meetings moving.

Once you know who to invite, it's time to spread the word!

The strategies below are great for letting students and families know about Science Club. I have never used them all at once because clubs fill up before I have had to. If you pick one or two that fit your campus, your science club will be full in no time.

Pro tip: Take good care of your school secretaries. Some registrations will filter through the front office. Some will just appear from parents passing through or from students and teachers who don't know what to do with them. It will be good for you if you have been treating the office staff well!

Getting the word out at Meet The Teacher night

Design Your Flier!

Nothing beats sending a regular old paper flier home. I like to make the top half an advertisement with details of the club (five *W*s again: who, what, when, where, and why), and the bottom half of the registration form a signed permission slip. When you are putting it together, try to format it so that you can send it home like a note, and it can also be taped up like a sign.

Paper works great because parents are used to receiving information this way, and it is obvious how they should respond. Printing on colored paper helps fliers stand out a little from the rest of the homework folder, but white works great. After typing your flier, print up enough sets to cover the classes that you'd like to invite and then pass them out to teachers to distribute in their classes. You should also e-mail the teachers to ask them nicely to pass them out. (Remember that stack of soccer-camp fliers you threw away last week?)

If making a large set of copies is difficult on your campus, cut the number of sheets in half by designing your flier as a half sheet. You can reduce the amount further by sending three or four fliers to each teacher and then use the morning announcements to alert any students interested in Science Club to ask their teacher for a flier.

Fliers should also be set up in high-traffic areas. An obvious place is the office, but I have also had good luck with setting up a table with fliers and a few cool specimens at Meet the Teacher Night or Open House. You can sit at the table to answer questions, or you can let the table speak for itself.

Building a Registration Sheet

Registration sheets are your chance to gather information that you need to manage the club. The information is likely available somewhere in the office, but if you ever need the information, it will be *much* easier for you if you have gathered the information beforehand, especially if you need it after the secretary has gone home or after the office has closed. At the end of the registration process, you should make a copy of the registration sheets you have received. That way you have one for your files and another set to keep in a notebook that travels with you to dismissal or to the playground for outside labs.

On my registration sheet, I ask for:

* Student name
* Grade
* Homeroom teacher
* Parent/guardian name
* Parent/guardian e-mail
* Parent/guardian phone number
* Alternate phone number
* Alternate emergency contact
* Allergies
* How student will be picked up
* Payment procedures

Phone Numbers

Having access to parent phone numbers is important if you ever have a member who isn't picked up after the meeting or if you need parental backup to deal with misbehavior. If your club is open to students across the campus, you won't have access to the contact information for students from other classes. You will need to gather that information just like you would for your own students at the beginning of the year.

PAYMENT

Whatever payment procedures you choose needs to be very clearly explained on the registration form. Besides telling families how to pay, you need to tell them how *not* to pay. In the years that parents pay directly, I tell families that payment is to be made in cash (no checks, IOUs, or money orders), and the money should be stapled directly to the registration sheet. With clear instructions, there are still going to be one or two people who don't get it right, but one or two is way better than a crowd.

ALLERGIES

Keep track of the allergies your members have! There are great labs out there that you will have to avoid if they present a danger. Parents may write in things like "pollen," "grass," or "seasonal" on the form, but I'm not worried about kids getting the sniffles. I have plenty of tissues.

I'm hunting for kids who might have *anaphylactic shock* that covers you in rashes, closes up your airway, and kills you. (Think peanut allergy.) There are plenty of things that kids can be allergic to. Besides nut allergies, I have had kids with shellfish, milk, egg, latex, citrus, and fish allergies. I even had a severe *pepper* allergy once.

Knowing about allergies in advance makes it easy to plan labs that won't kill your students, so be sure to keep track. If you ever meet a teacher who doesn't worry about allergies, you'll know they have never seen a student suffering from a reaction. I promise you that the best time to find out about Ben's latex allergy is *not* halfway through the balloon-rocket lab when twenty kids are chasing their windbags of death around the room.

DISMISSAL PROCEDURES

You should clearly state your expectations for how and when students get picked up after meetings. (I dismiss from the front of the school while parents stay in their cars.) Include the dismissal location and time and perhaps a statement that membership privileges are extended to families who pick up their student on time. Don't get much pushier than that on pickup times. Even if you are very clear about the time, you should still expect to wait with the last few members for about ten minutes. I usually call a parent after waiting ten minutes, but you get to set your own timing based on your own comfort level.

Pro tip: Don't let late parents get you down. If the extra waiting gets on your nerves, do what I did. I started taking the last few kids back to the lab to help me clean up. Kids like cleaning better than waiting, I like the extra help, and the time spent waiting for parents isn't lost for me anymore. I hang up a sign at the dismissal point that explains where we went, and I include the phone number telling parents how to call me when they get there. When I have a parent who picks up late every time, I just work it out that we'll be in the lab cleaning, and I don't even call them anymore.

Morning Announcements

Use morning announcements to let students know about Science Club. It's free advertising to a captive audience, and the system is already in place for delivering information that way. You *could* arrange to be down in the office to announce Science Club yourself over the loudspeaker, but I don't suggest that for several reasons:

1. You have to find somebody to watch your class while you go to the office.
2. Speaking over the loudspeaker is nerve-racking.
3. Kids have to hear the announcement for at least a week to remember it.

An easier way is to type up a script the way you'd like it to be read and then deliver it to the person who makes the announcements. He or she just adds it into the announcement rotation for however long you ask him or her to read it. Below is an example of a script that I have used in the past:

Science-Club Announcement to Be Read Daily during the Week of _____

Hey, science lovers,

Listen up! Our school is going to have an after-school science club starting soon! If you are interested in doing *real* science, like hunting meteorites, dissecting crustaceans, playing with bugs, and building a real fossil collection, you should join Science Club! We will meet on Tuesdays after school in the library, and anybody can join! Just have your parents sign you up with the blue registration sheet, and drop it off at the office! Or you can pick up a handout from your teacher or print one off from the school website. When Science Club is full, we won't be able to sign anybody else up, so write yourself a note in your homework folder right now. See you at Science Club! Teachers, the blue Science Club forms have been placed in your mailbox. If you need more, Mrs. Meyer has extras in her room. Thanks!

Campus Websites

If your school has a website, include information about your science club! Ask the person who maintains the website to include the science-club flier on the website. This gets the word out to families who have had their fliers "mysteriously disappear" between home and school. Also, if somebody e-mails you for information, you can direct him or her to a flier.

Pro tip: If you are already making arrangements with the website manager, go ahead and ask him or her to post your donation wish list of soda bottles, yarn, and broken appliances that you need for Science Club.

Depending on your technology skills, you may decide to upgrade and make the registration into an electronic form that is submitted online. That is a fine way to go, but definitely not required. Only do that if it makes your life *easier*. You should still keep paper registration as an option, because even though you could probably recruit a full club using just the school website and social media, the students who benefit most from Science Club will be cut out of the process if their family doesn't have a computer.

Social Media

Many schools have a presence on Facebook, Twitter, or other social media. If your school does, arrange to have the science-club information posted. If your roster still has room a week later, have it posted again.

These sites are also a great way to get good public relations going for your school once Science Club has started. Posting pictures of cool science projects is a fun way to show the great things that are happening on campus. Principals and parents *love* to see that sort of thing. Check with your administrator or handbook to learn the procedures for documenting student achievements with pictures and how to submit those photos to the person responsible for managing social media. (Remember to tag your science-club pictures and posts with the hashtag #TSCHB (The Science Club Handbook) so you can connect with other science-club leaders.!)

Posting Signs

Hanging up signs is another good way to get the message out. If your flier has the right format, you don't need to create a sign; just post the flier in high-traffic areas. The best places are on the inside and outside of the front door, above water fountains, on bulletin boards, and on the inside doors of the restroom stalls. You can also post them on the walls in the hall, but most folks will not turn their heads to read them.

You can order big plastic yard signs and post them in front of the school. (I get mine from Vistaprint, eSigns, or Staples.) These are a good way to catch the attention of parents driving by. If you decide to order some, keep your message short enough that parents can read the whole thing in two seconds or less. Nobody pulls over to read a paragraph. Limit it to less than eight words, and *make them big.* I don't suggest spending money on printed signs in the beginning because the response is slower than with fliers. I only started doing that whenever I developed a good science-club budget. If you are itching to post signs immediately and the fliers aren't exciting enough for you, just copy the cheerleaders and turn your first meeting into a poster-making party.

Video Announcements

One year I hit upon the idea of making a little video I would e-mail to teachers to show to their homeroom classes. With absolutely zero experience making video commercials, I knew that creativity would be the only asset that I had in my favor. I got dressed up in a really stuffy collar and tie and read my lines directly into the camera with the most dreadful, boring and monotone voice I could muster. At the very end of the twenty-second snooze fest, my fellow teacher standing out of view dashed a bucket of water into my face. It was ridiculous, and it worked. I sent the video link to the campus and asked teachers to show their kids. The splash took them by such a surprise that most classes watched it several times just for the chuckle.

You don't have to know anything about video to put together a little commercial. Just use your phone and get someone to film you doing your thing. You can add the video link to your website, ask the librarian to show it to the students who rotate through, or attach it to a QR code to hang outside your door. Another nice thing about video is that once you film it, it doesn't get thrown away like the fliers or blown down like the signs. It just keeps on working for you.

CLOSING REGISTRATION

If everything goes as planned, your club will fill quickly. You need to plan what you will do when the club is full so you don't end up with 150 kids signed up!

When your roster is full, stop accepting registrations, and start a waiting list. Turning people away is difficult, but it is much better than stuffing a club so full of kids that you can't manage it. In the beginning, I really hated seeing the disappointed faces when kids heard that Science Club was full, so I collected the extra registrations, called their families, and gave them another option.

The other option was to open a second section of Science Club. After the Tuesday club filled, I opened a Thursday club, and it filled just as quickly. The upside was that twice as many students enjoyed Science Club that year, and materials were cheaper because of buying in bulk. The downsides were that I doubled my Science Club workload, lost a second afternoon each week, and still ended up turning people away once the second club filled. I decided to avoid burnout after that by halting registrations when the clubs fill. Now I only register a second club if another teacher leads it.

CHAPTER 4

First-Meeting Procedures and Expectations

● ● ●

IT'S IMPORTANT TO TEACH STUDENTS your procedures and expectations up front. It may seem tiresome to explain procedures when everyone is itching to do science, but the explanations will be *time well spent.* Consider how many different ways students are trained to get a drink when they are thirsty:

- They might raise their hand and ask to go.
- They might shout out their request.
- They might hold up the sign-language *W* for water.
- They might stand up and look around for a water fountain.
- They might flip over a colored cup on their desk.
- They might walk out of your room.
- They might say nothing and wait for the end of class.
- They might ask to go to the restroom and then sneak a drink instead.
- They might pull out a water bottle and start drinking at their desk.

If you don't explain your own procedures, students will revert to the one from their normal class, or they'll invent their own. Whatever procedures you choose should be clearly explained up front, and possibly even practiced and role-played. It will stream-line the meetings throughout the year and will save everyone lots of time and anxiety.

Even if the school year has been going for several months, your first meeting will be the first time that group gathers under your guidance. Treat the first meeting just like the first day of school. It's your best chance to have everybody's attention to explain meeting expectations and procedures. Remember to take advantage of your attentive audience! Curiosity about the club and uncertainty about what to expect will keep everyone much more focused than usual. Members will come in quieter and more open to your guidance than at any other time. Take advantage of that quiet, because it won't happen again until the first meeting of your next science club.

ARRIVAL PROCEDURES

Arriving at Science Club happens in *two stages*. The first stage is when students arrive at your door, and the second stage is when they come into your room.

I teach members what to do when they get to my door, because when they arrive, I'll still be handling dismissal for my regular class. I will be managing an end-of-the-day problem, talking to a parent, or cleaning up from my classroom instruction. Sometimes I'll be heading to the teacher's-lounge refrigerator to pick up specimens for the meeting. Members need to know *exactly* what to do when they arrive. If they aren't trained, they will have a party or a riot in the hallway just outside the door.

My procedure is for the students to come to my door, sit down in a line in the hallway, and wait until I invite them in. They know that sitting is a requirement, and only students who are sitting quietly get invited in. That training is a huge help when I have to run to the office for a fast conference call or go find a missing student on the bus. My science-club members will be hanging out outside my door waiting on me when I get back.

This procedure is public enough that it trains other teachers what Science Club members should be doing. If they see Science Club kids arrive and sit quietly each week, they'll start to expect it. If Mr. Hyperactive and Ms. Runandsqueal start a game of tag while waiting for me, those teachers will be comfortable reminding them to sit down and hush.

The procedure for students entering my room is to put away backpacks, find the student's name tag (see below), and take a seat. You decide whether students choose their own seats or if you assign them. I usually choose their seats by laying out name tags on the desks where I want them to sit. When students come in, they have to sit down at their name tag and put it on their shirt where I can see it.

As students arrive, they will be carrying backpacks, jackets, lunch boxes, school projects, and any number of other things. Normally, students entering your class will have access to a locker or coat hook, but since Science Club members are usually from all different classes, they won't have these storage areas during meetings. If you don't have a plan for that pile of twenty-five backpacks and jackets, you will get buried in it.

The best solution that I have found is to have students leave their backpacks in a line against the wall in the hallway outside my classroom. That way, there isn't a large stack in the back of the classroom, and when we dismiss, everybody can walk straight to their bag.

If there isn't room in the hallway, I designate a corner of the room to stack bags, and they hang their jackets on their chairs. This works fine, but I only let a few students at a time pick up their bags at the end so there isn't a mad rush into the bag pile.

Should You Use Name Tags?

Name tags are a wonderful thing, and I'm always surprised that more teachers don't use them. You can manage a club just fine without them, but they are such a great tool that I don't know why you would. I use the plastic-sleeve name tags that attach with a little safety pin attached to the back, and I reuse the sleeves each year. Many teachers remember names easily (I don't), so they see creating name tags as an unnecessary task. What they don't know is that name tags are so much more than that. Name tags are helpful for:

Opening a meeting. "Find and sit" is a great opening procedure to get everyone focused for the meeting. After I lay out tags where I want them, students take a minute to find their own tag, put it on, and get comfortable with their seat mates for the day. Separating and combining groups in new ways is easy, and making adjustments is as quick as moving the tags around.

Attendance. After the students arrive, taking attendance is a breeze. Just pick up the unclaimed tags, and you'll know who is absent. Or even better, assign that job to a student, and have him or her deliver the leftover tags to you.

Classroom management. There is something magical about using someone's name during instruction. You can easily include the quiet kids and handily manage the not so quiet. It won't matter if you forget the names of kids you see only once a week. Their names will be plastered to their shirts. Even better, after a few meetings with name tags, everyone's names will be firmly in your head! The tags are a great stress reliever when you have a sub for Science Club. Your replacement will instantly know everyone's name.

Notes, allergies, and phone numbers. Using the pin-on tags lets me use the back of name tags for student-specific information.

Students who have a serious allergy can have that noted. Seating reminders or accomplishments in Science Club can also be recorded. Any sort of special instruction that is unique to a student can be recorded on the back of his or her tag, and it's a great place to write parent phone numbers for easy access at the end of the day. Just keep in mind that name tags aren't private, so don't write anything on there that shouldn't be public knowledge.

Dismissal. At the end of meetings, name tags become a physical checklist of departing students. Each student's tag has his or her destination written on it (i.e., after-school childcare, walk home, mom's classroom, or parent pickup). I can look quickly at each member's tag and see where he or she will be going. After I have released the walkers and teachers' kids, I walk my quiet line of "parent pickup" students to the front door. Members then *sit* in front of the school. They *stay seated*, and when they see their ride, they hold their name tag up in the air. I take it from them, and they stand up and leave. This procedure prevents twenty-five students from rushing away at once, leaving me behind, wondering where each student went. At the end, every tag in my hand is a student I released to his or her parents.

Potty Training Your Scientists

As students travel from their classrooms to Science Club, they should use the restroom if they can. (Hopefully in the actual restroom.) Also, during that first five minutes, students will be arriving a few at a time, so it is the perfect chance for students to step out to use the facilities. The more students who remember to go before the lab begins, the fewer the interruptions from students needing to leave in the middle of the meeting. In my clubs, students just raise their hands and ask, and I let them go. Science Club is interesting enough that if a student asks to go, he or she really needs to go, and I always let the student go immediately.

Let your students know your expectations for how they should ask to go to the restroom. I have them raise their hands and go with permission (which I always give). That way I know who is out of the room, and they can go whenever they need to. Students are excited to be at Science Club, so the chances they are asking for a break just because they are bored are pretty small. And if they are bored enough to need an elimination vacation, I don't really mind. It is Science Club, after all. You won't know these students as well as your normal class, so consider being more lenient just to save yourself from kindergartner accidents.

One limitation that I *do* put on restroom breaks is that I only let one boy and one girl go at a time. There is no limit to the shenanigans that can happen with friends in the bathroom when they are armed with markers, raw eggs, a balloon, and duct tape.

Show-and-Tell

Show-and-tell has not always been part of my meetings, but luckily, one smart student changed that. During Science Club one year, a third grader named Violet joined and began to attend regularly. She was *always* looking for ways to make meetings more exciting. She would sneak in games to play, create works of art from the lab supplies, and tell silly jokes just to keep things hopping. It was pretty normal for her to be "creating her own path" in Science Club. One afternoon, she raised her hand and announced we needed to start having show-and-tell in Science Club, and she was going to start us off. She whipped a dead bird's wing and a plastic bag full of mud out of her backpack, started giving a speech about them, and ended up with the rest of the group totally enthralled by her specimens. In two minutes, she totally changed Science Club procedures.

From that moment on, show-and-tell became a forum for students to show off the cool things that they have collected over time. We designated the first five minutes of every meeting to show-and-tell, and everybody wanted a turn. We had some really interesting rocks, a preserved sheep, and some seashells, but after a few weeks, we started to hit turbulence. It got a little chaotic, so we put in place two requirements for presenting at show-and-tell, and it has been smooth sailing ever since:

Requirement 1. Your specimen must be related to science in some way.

Kindergartner Gabe helped us establish this requirement. One day during show-and-tell, he decided that getting his chance to present was his most important goal in life. He just might die if he didn't have a turn. He started waving his hands to be called on as if he was stuck in the middle of the ocean, trying to catch the eye of a search plane. After a not-so-subtle barrage of "Oooooo oooooo oooooo!" didn't work, he strengthened his campaign with a desperately bellowed *"Pick meeee!"* I finally gave in and called on him to present. It was only then that we both realized that he hadn't actually brought something to show. After a desperate assessment of every item within his reach, he ripped off one of his shoes and gave us an impromptu presentation on why it was so smelly.

Impressive, but not what I had in mind. After that, I insisted that objects be directly related to science. I know that anything (including smelly shoes) can be related to science, but sometimes the connection is so thin that I disallow an object on principle.

Requirement 2. Your specimen must be on your desk at the start of the meeting.

Arriving at Science Club is an exciting time! It's fun to visit with friends, it's interesting to check out the day's lab, and it's a great time to shake off the confines of the regular school day. This energy often distracts kids from getting their jar of wiggly worms out and ready to present. Sometimes kids don't even have something to show, but like Gabe, they are confident that they can find something worth talking about in their backpacks.

We would get halfway through the opening presentation when a handful of kids would hop up, sprint for the backpacks and start burrowing around, trying to find a moldy sandwich or a dinosaur toy from recess. Of course, they would miss the current presentation, and the other kids would be distracted by watching the minor miners hunting for the worms that had escaped into their bags during the day.

To smooth the process, members are now required to have their show-and-tell item ready on top of their desk when the meeting begins. That makes the process go much faster, it gives the table groups something to talk about while they wait for us to get started, and it gives me a chance to quickly approve the specimens.

Show-and-tell has become a favorite part of our science club's activities, and I encourage you to give it a try.

BEHAVIOR EXPECTATIONS

News flash! You can stop fighting your students to make them engage! Students are desperate to participate in the labs, so the normal burden of motivating students is gone. High-interest activities are *great* at reducing student misbehaviors. Students who get wild in class to fight their boredom will toss their tricks aside when the catapults come out. Petty arguments will be vaporized when the dry ice starts steaming. You won't have to manage boredom battles because you won't have any bored kids left!

It will be a relief to be free from those old habits. It's time to shift your classroom-management skills from constantly redirecting kids who act silly for entertainment to guiding the group's enthusiasm in way that moves learning forward. You will need a few procedures to help you manage the excitement.

LISTENING SKILLS

During meetings, there will be *lots* of visiting with friends, discussing experiments, and talking about cool science videos just posted online. You will need a way to put the brakes on the talking, and the only way it will happen is if you explain clearly what you expect. Explain how students should listen to teacher instructions and to other student presentations. My procedure involves holding up my hand quietly and waiting until the group copies me, but you can use whatever procedure fits your campus.

I also make my club a *no interruption zone.* The enthusiasm that forms in students during meetings often spurs them to interject into the middle of presentations or instructions. I love the engagement, but meetings are much better now that I push back against interrupting other people when they are sharing with the class. You can decide how strict to be in that area. In my club, raising hands in the middle of a presentation is interrupting—save questions until the end!

Hands on Your Own Project

In the regular classroom, I expect students to keep their hands to themselves so they don't irritate the helicopter parents eagerly waiting for a story about how their baby is getting mistreated in class. In Science Club, I expect students to keep their hands *on their own projects* so that they don't slow each other's progress. It's tempting for students to "fix" somebody else's project when they get a chance to show off what they know, but if they aren't invited, it's hands off.

The amount of investment and ownership students feel over their projects is much higher than a regular class assignment. If another student starts to make adjustments or "repairs" without an invite, it can create tension even if they are good friends. It's easier to maintain this expectation than to deal with arguments and damaged projects.

Treat Each Other Kindly

You won't need a laundry list of behavior expectations about how to work together. As long as members are expected to treat each other kindly, things will work out well. The expectation is easy to remember, easy to enforce, and it covers every interaction between students.

Any Questions? (Not Stories)

During meetings, after the lab is explained to the group, hands will start popping up with questions. It's important to answer the legitimate questions that come up, but teach members that this is not story time. It's tempting (especially for younger students) to keep the club waiting while they tell a story that popped into their mind while you were giving instructions:

"My gramma gave me a purple rock, and I saw one just like it on TV, and now I have a rock collection, and my dad says that rocks belong outside, but I hide them under my bed, anyway."

It's your call on how strict to be, but story time can catch on fast, and ten kids will be waving their hands, wanting to tell you a story. I ask them to save it until the lab begins and tell it to me then.

No More "What If"

Some students are fond of using "what if" questions during the question and answer time just to hear themselves speak. These are just a passive way of getting *you* to tell a story of what *could* happen. "What ifs" rarely move the lab forward, and they usually just waste time by getting the teacher to talk or by getting a giggle from friends:

- "What if the crawfish pinches my finger and I scream, and the crawfish poops?"
- "What if all twenty balloons pop in my face before I get them tied onto their strings?"
- "What if I drop my mirror and it breaks, and a piece cuts my toe, and kids start fainting, and I throw up, and..."

If a member wants to talk about his or her "what if" question *after* the lab has started, I'm fine with that, but he or she usually chooses to start working on the lab once the potential audience has turned attention away from the Q&A.

Note. "What if" questions in this context are questions that students are asking the teacher to talk about, not questions that students might ask during an investigation or exploration. Asking themselves a "what if" during an investigation is great!

SNACKS

Some kids need to munch. Students headed home after school are usually accustomed to eating a snack soon after dismissal. I don't provide a snack for students, but I do allow them to bring one if they want to. Allowing them to continue that habit has a couple of benefits:

1. They'll be happier with their blood-sugar levels raised.
2. Snacking gives them something to do while waiting for the meeting to start.
3. Their mouths will be full, so it is easier for you to give instructions.

If you decide to provide snack for your science club, *keep it simple* (like Cheerios in a paper cup), remember it in your budget, and assign the snack job to a couple of students so you don't spend half the meeting passing out munchies. Providing a regular snack to twenty-five kids is a pretty daunting task, so think twice before you commit to it.

Introductions: Getting to Know Each Other

After procedures and expectations, warm things up by letting everyone introduce themselves. Perhaps share name, grade, and favorite movie/ice cream/book. This will help kids feel more comfortable with the group and will help everyone get to know each other. If time allows, you can play an icebreaker game. If you have a favorite, use it. If you can't think of one, play Two Truths and a Lie.

Two Truths and a Lie

You can play with a whole class or in small groups. Small groups are faster, but not as many people interact with each other. Explain the following game to the students, and then give them a moment to think.

The first person shares three statements with the group. Two of the statements should be the truth, and one of them is a lie. I might say:

1. I've gone swimming in a lake full of piranhas.
2. I have parachuted out of a plane at ten thousand feet.
3. I have been chased by an octopus.

After making the statements, the group votes on which one they think is the lie. It's a fun way to find out about each other and a good way for you to assess the group. You'll learn which students are too shy to participate, which ones are creative liars, which ones have led interesting lives, and which ones can follow instructions with multiple steps.

(By the way, I wasn't chased by the octopus. It just sat on the reef staring at me.)

CLEANUP

Mud, glitter vinegar and baking soda, blenders and bubbles—some of the best labs happen in the midst of a giant mess. Messes are *not* against the rules in Science Club, but leaving messes for somebody else is. To manage chaos without tearing out your hair, train members that at cleanup time, every member handles his or her own mess and *then* helps members close by with their mess until the room is clean. Everybody *keeps working* until the room is ready.

In practice, the best way to get students moving for cleanup is to assign specific tasks to specific people or groups. For example, you could say, "Katy, please gather all the markers for me. Erin, throw away all the leftover scraps of paper. Jeff, please make sure that the floors are dry. Group two will dry off the table tops, and everybody else puts away the equipment. Ready, go!"

Pro tip: If cleanup is going to make you two minutes late for dismissal, *be late for dismissal.* The amount of mess that takes two minutes for the whole group will take you forty minutes if you do it by yourself after they leave.

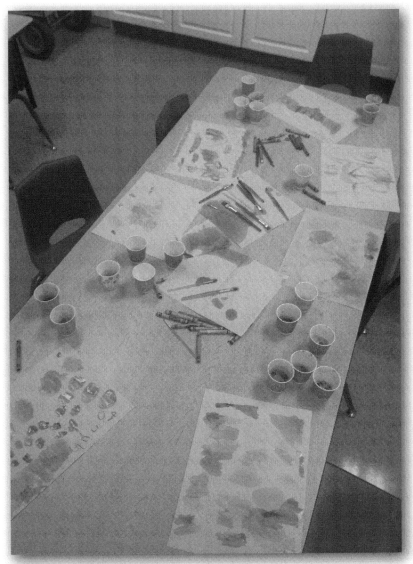

Big messes can mean big learning. Be ready to
accommodate splashes and sprinkles!

DISMISSAL PROCEDURES

Wouldn't it be great if students already knew how to gather backpacks, line up, and walk out calmly? *Fat chance.* If you don't train members how dismissal works, the *best*-case scenario is that each member's homeroom teacher has trained the students perfectly on how to behave during dismissal. Even if they have, though, you will still have ten different behaviors coming from ten different homerooms.

In the *worst*-case scenario, the bell rings, students stage a sixty-second riot, and then the older students trample the younger students as they sprint for the door. Thirty minutes after the stampede, you will get a phone call from Bailey's mother wondering where he is. After a desperate search, you find him drawing rude pictures in the bathroom. Of course, Bailey's mother will need to arrange a meeting to yell at you for not understanding her son's artistic side.

Don't do that to yourself. You need to train members how *your* dismissal procedures work *before* the actual dismissal. At the first meeting, take five minutes to teach the students what dismissal looks like. Walk them through it just as you would on the first day of school. And in a couple of months (or next week) when they forget how to do it, just train them again. (The procedure that I use is explained in the Name Tag section.)

Pro tip: Be late at dismissal. It is *much* easier to manage dismissal if you are two minutes late to the front door. It gives parents a few extra minutes to arrive so that when you get to the front door, students leave immediately. Arriving at the front door exactly on time will be a challenge for both you and the parents. You will usually be a little early or a little late. Be late. If you are stuck waiting, you will be busy managing twenty excitable scientists with projects, backpacks, lunch boxes, and full bladders. If parents are stuck waiting, they will be managing the music and air temperature in their car.

CHAPTER 5

Planning Your Meeting Topics

● ● ●

Science is curiosity that gets acted upon.

—James Cameron, Explorer

Planning topics for your meetings will be based on what you need out of a science club. If your goals are specific, you can target specific content. If your mission is enjoyment, that will be easy enough, too.

In my earliest science clubs, I flew by the seat of my pants when planning. I had a well-stocked lab from the teacher before me, I had a budget available to spend on supplies with short notice, and I had a principal who let me plan meetings however I wanted to. It was easy to drop by the fish market the night before and pick up a class set of octopus, crabs, fish, or snails. In the mornings before meetings, I would look up information about that species and perhaps preview a YouTube video or two about it. (See below for why you should *always preview the videos.*) At the meeting, I would roll it all out to the kids. The kids and I enjoyed it, and they were definitely learning interesting things. This strategy worked pretty well, and if you decide to manage your club this way, you'll get some pretty great meetings out of it.

After several semesters, I starting feeling as if we were missing some great experiences that we could have with a little more preparation and planning. I wanted to make holograms and launching rockets, but those don't just happen with ten minutes of shopping or a run to the supply closet. They require a bit of research, a bit of planning, and a bit of hunting for just the right supplies. *The results of the extra efforts turned out to be more than worth it.* Students were totally taken in by the sorcery of acids and bases. They were so excited about their mealworm habitats that they took them home and rebuilt them into little bug apartment buildings.

The extra efforts sharpened my skills as well. After testing ambitious projects in Science Club, it was easy to integrate them into my normal instruction. My ability to identify meaningful activities grew, and planning became more enjoyable. Best of all, my personal identity shifted from a tired teacher to an excited science lover.

In the last section of this handbook is a collection of ten labs I have used in science clubs. They have worked well in the past, and they will be a great starting point for your group, but don't limit yourself to these labs! Once you start a club, activities and opportunities for cool labs will begin to appear, and you should definitely take advantage of them.

Always Preview the Videos!

I have a teacher friend who enjoys a tradition with her third-grade class to get into the holiday spirit every year. As students get antsy with vacation anticipation, she will squeeze one more lesson out of them by reading *The Grinch That Stole Christmas* with the class. One year she decided that it would be easier to find a YouTube video of someone reading the book, and she could use her projector to show the video. With the video doing the work, she could walk around the room, monitor the readers, and enjoy the story herself. When the time came, she did a quick search and found a good-looking video with a pleasant-sounding narrator. She turned up the sound and began patrolling the room to make sure everyone was 100 percent focused on the story of Cindy Lou Who. She didn't have to apply much pressure on the kids, though, because the narrator did a great job. He read so well that not a single student missed it when the reader improvised the last line with, *"and that f#(<!#& Grinch."* In the end, the students gave high marks to the production, but they didn't rate it quite as high as the track-and-field performance by their teacher as she hurdled desks and chairs, sprinting to the front to kill the speakers.

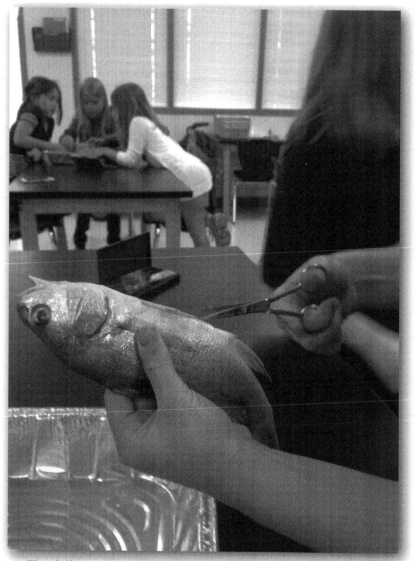

Ten dollars at the fish market catapulted this elementary Science Club lab past the experiences of most high school Biology students.

Choose Science: Avoid Models

When you are planning your labs, real-life experiences rule. Kids should use their senses as much as possible. Kids need a real frog, not another frog life-cycle model. They don't need to color and label a paper puzzle of a lobster; they need to touch, sniff, and open up a *real* lobster.

Models Are Not Science—They Just Explain Science

They are a physical metaphor to help kids understand what you're saying, and they're boring. Sometimes you do have to use them if the real science is out of reach. There are plenty of solar system, rock cycle, and plant models out there. You probably don't have the budget for a field trip to the moon, the time for a voyage to Hawaii, or the motivation to study smallpox very closely. In instances where money, time, or motivation are in short supply, you can limp the lesson along with a model. Just keep in mind that *models are a crutch*, and they are never as much fun as seeing "the real thing."

Teachers who substitute arts and crafts models for real science usually forget how to play with balloons, catch frogs, collect bugs, or start a rock collection. When their students get bored from the constant barrage of cutting, gluing, and filling in the blanks, both the teacher and students start to think they dislike science. *Wrong.* They just dislike being bored.

The good news is that you can rescue your students from this boredom coma and protect yourself from the hoard of drooling zombies. Using *real* science saves your classroom from the drudgery of another insect life-cycle chart. Mealworms are cheap, and they don't bite.

Don't be intimidated by concepts that you are uncomfortable with, like dissection, rocketry, or spiders. There is an incredible amount of concrete learning that can happen with simple supplies like toothpicks, string, soda bottles, or rubber bands. With a roll of tape and some recycled newspaper, kids can stay busy studying architecture for hours.

EMBRACE THE CLASSICS!

There are a few labs that have developed the reputation of over-used clichés in science class. Baking soda and vinegar volcanoes, growing bread mold, sprouting beans, and butterfly labs are all so familiar to science teachers that those topics are often banned from science fairs. Teachers don't want to bore the kids, so they keep reinventing the wheel with new labs. New lab topics are great, but there is no need to avoid labs that have been done before.

I used to work hard putting together brand-new labs every week. Thank goodness the kids straightened me out. They got tired of waiting and just started asking me for the labs they'd heard about for so long.

Even though I've seen way too many volcanoes, most of my students were still waiting to see one. And the few students who had already seen one were eager to do it again. Volcanoes aren't a cliché; they are a classic.

Find Your Science Dealers

Reading teachers have libraries, history teachers have museums, and the gym coach can visit the health and fitness store, but where should science teachers gather their supplies from? When you are starting out, it's tricky figuring out where to start.

You can go online to shop, but what if you need materials now? What if you need to touch the supplies before you spend the money? There isn't a Science "R" Us on any corner in my town. Luckily, there are resources that are just as good. Besides the regular grocery store, consider the following:

Restaurant-Supply Stores

Restaurant-supply stores have tons of lab equipment for cheap. Food science (a.k.a. cooking) requires all the scales, bins, beakers, trays, buckets, scrapers, knives, and takeout boxes you'll ever need. They are nearly always open to the public, and even if they aren't, they'll usually accommodate teachers. Restaurant owners can be even poorer than teachers, so supplies can't be priced sky-high like in those expensive science catalogs that constantly show up in your mailbox.

Hardware Stores

Home Depot, Lowes, and any other hardware store out there will have heaps of raw materials available for labs and projects. Boards, bolts, nails, sand, seeds, rocks, pipes, light bulbs, and rope are all available for the brave.

Just last week I planned a lab where students built butterfly nets, and I needed affordable handles for 230 kids. I found them at Lowes in the concrete section (eighteen-inch wooden stakes were way cheaper than dowel rods or PVC pipe).

Don't be scared of the hardware store! If you don't understand which hardware you need, just ask an employee. Think of the store as a library and the staff as librarians of building and fixing. They'll help you figure it out!

Grocery Stores (with Names You Can't Pronounce)

Need a pig uterus or a package of duck skulls for your lab? How about a catfish as big as your arm? Your regular grocery store (whatever it might be) will have plenty of supplies. In fact, you could probably run your science club program for the whole year just out of that one store. But if you want to take the interest levels up a notch, visit a grocery store that you or your students don't normally shop in.

My local Walmart doesn't have the whole fish, kidneys, durian, or seaweed that my local Asian market does. It doesn't have the whole cow tongues, cacti, and pig heads that my local *carniceria* (butcher's shop) does. By visiting stores where I encounter new products, I can easily provide exciting new science topics to my scientists.

I imagine the same idea would work for the science club whose families shop exclusively at the *carniceria*. If they visited my local Albertsons, there'd be specimens they could try for the first time. The key is in cultivating high interest through new experiences. If you've never seen a seedless watermelon, the first time you eat one, you'll be impressed. (I know because I predate those delicious lumps of genetically modified goodness.)

Find Your Science-Club Friends!

All around the world, there are other educators working hard to deliver great science to their students. Not long ago, they worked mostly in isolation, but with today's social media options, you can easily find people working on the same things you are! On Twitter, Facebook, Instagram, and most other platforms, you can tag your posts with hashtags to help people find your content. If you get pictures of a lab that goes really well (or if it goes horribly wrong too), then post those pictures along with the hashtag **#TSCHB** so other members of our science-club community will find you. You can also search that same hashtag to gather great lab ideas from your peers!

CHAPTER 6

Hacking Your Club for High Performance

● ● ●

HACKS MAKE LIFE EASIER! THE word *hack* has a bad reputation. To some folks, it means invading computers or stealing data. In reality, hacking means finding useful shortcuts or strategies to make a process easier. Any time a strategy makes my job easier *while* increasing learning, I'm all over it.

This chapter has a great collection of strategies to increase student engagement and make classroom management easier. Each one *increases* student productivity while *decreasing* your stress level.

As a science-club hacker, you'll learn how to:

- Quickly erase huge messes
- Motivate students with magic words
- Manage behavior with a single Magical Mantra
- Empower exploration with a single word
- Create perfect timing for transitions
- How to install a "pause button" in your lab
- Use the Know-It-All kid as your public relations representative
- Move your troops easily from place to place
- Quiet a crowd easily

Magic Words

The first set of hacks is the magic words. Use magic words in Science Club (or your classroom) to amp up the learning. Their power may seem too good to be true, but when you wave your magic wand over the crowd, you'll be surprised how much power you have. Remember to use your powers for good!

"That's Interesting. How Did You Do That?"

How many of us have suffered through a professional development where the presenter insists we transform students into self-motivated learners? And how many of us walked out at the end with no idea how to make that happen? OK, everyone, put your hands down.

This phrase is so simple that it seems almost trite. But lurking beneath the surface is the power to create self-motivated students who charge forward in their own learning. If you still haven't had a chance to watch the TED Talk video by Sugata Mitra titled "The Child-Driven Education," *go do it now*! Listen to it on your headphones or on your school computer. Whatever—just do it.

In the video, you'll learn how students who pursue their own projects are good at learning already, but when an interested adult uses the phrase *That's interesting*, students get validation for their efforts. (There isn't a value judgment as if you said, "That's great!" or "Good job!") When it is combined with *How did you do that?* students begin to evaluate their own work and to communicate their own progress. Students become more invested in their own learning than if a teacher is providing feedback or using rewards to push them through the learning. They also get stronger at monitoring their own progress.

As students receive validation and hone self-monitoring skills, it's easier for them to enjoy the learning process and to set their own learning goals.

The best part of this strategy is that *anybody* can use it. In the TED talk, Dr. Mitra names this hack "the method of the grand-mother" because even if Grandma doesn't understand what a child is drawing, she'll still act interested, and the child will keep drawing excitedly.

"THAT'S A GOOD QUESTION. HOW CAN WE FIND THE ANSWER?"

Years ago, I was hired as an ethnographer in the Fort Worth Museum of Science and History. (*Ethno* means "culture," and *graph* means "write.") My job was to quietly observe visitors in a new exhibit and to determine which elements visitors engaged with easily, which elements didn't attract people, and what the differences were between the two. It was interesting work, and it was good practice for me to see what motivated people to play. I spent dozens of hours stalking and documenting visitors, and we did make some improvements to the exhibit, but the single most valuable observation during the entire month was the experience of two brothers and their dad.

One of the more popular sections of the exhibit held a small, manipulative puzzle for guests to play with. (The word *manipulative* was used to mean moving pieces around to challenge your brain, not *manipulative* as in making you abandon all your other puzzle friends just so that you can spend all your time sucking up to the one puzzle that seeks constant validation by putting itself into an artificially superior position.)

One day, a six-year-old boy discovered the puzzle and began examining the pieces. He moved them this way and that, trying different solutions. After ten minutes, he sat down on the stool as if he was going to stay awhile. Ten minutes after that, his four-year-old brother brought over a stool and joined him. Those two brothers took turns moving the pieces, handing the puzzle back and forth, strategizing, testing, and rethinking. It was remarkable watching them focus on their work, because even in a science museum, it is uncommon to see a six-year-old stay that focused on a single artifact, much less his four-year-old brother. *At the thirty-minute mark, they showed no signs of slowing down!*

They started going back to retest old theories, they tried recalling past experiences, and they even tried brainstorming odd solutions that might help them find a breakthrough. Basically, they were learning in the most meaningful, collaborative, and self-motivated way possible. At the forty-five-minute mark, they were still going strong when their dad wandered over. The boys invited him to help, and he began examining the puzzle with them. It took him less than thirty seconds to solve it. Receiving an "answer" gave those boys immediate license to end their experiments. Thirty seconds after that, they had all disengaged from the puzzle and moved on to other activities, satisfied that they had "finished" the puzzle. It was the most remarkable and abrupt end to meaningful learning that I have ever seen.

I'm sure that dad didn't take time to visit a museum just to stop his boys from learning. But in handing over the answer to their question, *he robbed them of their exploration.* He removed the itch that they were trying to scratch, and there was no reason left for them to pursue their investigation.

In Science Club, there will be plenty of questions from members. Some of them you might even know the answer to! Don't let your own knowledge get in the way of student learning. Instead, cast a science spell on them. Just pull out your magic wand, and mutter the incantation, "That's a good question. How can we find the answer?" It will focus the young scientists and will make their brains itch so bad for answers, they'll sprint back to their seats and keep working.

MAGICAL MANTRA FOR MANAGING MEMBERS

Teachers recognize a tension between keeping enough control over a class to be productive and handing over enough control to the students to motivate engagement. This tension is especially noticeable when you lead an excited group of friends who aren't being graded through the dissections, rocket launches, and experiments with acid. The kids want to have fun, and you want everyone to stay alive and hopefully learn something. You can't surrender to anarchy, but if you manage your troops like a drill sergeant, they'll tune you out or leave.

How do you find that happy middle ground of controlled excitement? You use the Magical Mantra for managing members:

"I do science with kids who follow directions and who are good listeners."

The mantra lets students know what you are up to and what they need to do to be part of the labs. I *really* emphasize the mantra at the beginning of programs, because it's what I use for most of my redirection during labs. When students get off task or stop participating the right way, I don't lecture them or boss them around very much. I just say the mantra. If it doesn't take effect quickly, I pick up a key part of their lab equipment, utter the mantra again, and walk away for about thirty seconds. It doesn't take much longer than that to turn the toad into a scientist.

With the Magical Mantra, there isn't anything for kids to argue with. You aren't telling them to do anything, so it doesn't provide any opportunity for defiance or noncompliance. You are simply setting up the framework for how awesome science fun happens in your magical lair. Just keep in mind that the magic that powers the mantra is the fact your activity is fun and engaging. If your game is lame, kids won't give two shakes who you do science with.

"Yes"

This is the most powerful of the magic words. It can transform bored, slack-jawed students into goggle-wearing, rocket-launching, theory-testing scientists. It can also change you from flowery-dress- or plaid-tie-wearing milk sipper to fearless science seeker always on the lookout for the next spider-infested volcano to study, perhaps with the camera drone that your kids built at the last meeting.

Often teachers will focus and confine a class to one objective at a time to maintain control over content. Requests from students to explore other objectives are often denied in order to keep the class flowing in the right direction. It's hard to be accountable for content that you don't manage and control, so teachers tightly manage it instead. The idea is that if you let a kid explore whatever he or she wants, you lose control over where he or she ends up, and the other students will end up distracted. Students who would enjoy opportunities to explore new content areas quickly become accustomed to hearing *no*.

Project-based learning, inquiry-based instruction, and open-ended rubrics are all great tools for *easing* the limitations of normal instruction, *but they are still bounded by the content objectives*. If your unit is on force and motion, you can plan the best inquiry lab in town, but you'll still be focusing on force and motion.

Science Club removes the pressure to restrict content. Students enjoy the freedom to explore and discover based on their interests. The next time a student asks permission to throw their airplane off the balcony, put slime in the freezer, or smash their fossil to see what's inside, watch their eyes light up when you tell them *yes*! And don't forget to pat yourself on the back when they bring their results back to class.

CANARY KIDS

Transitioning from one portion of a lesson to the next requires timing. One skill of a talented teacher is the ability to figure out when to start that transition. If a teacher lets the first portion go too long, kids get bored and start to fidget, and the teacher has to struggle to draw their attention back to the lesson. If the teacher transitions too early, students will miss out on parts of the learning that should have happened, and they might not be prepared for the next step.

It's a similar situation to the coal miners long ago. As the miners dug the coal out of the mine, they had to be constantly aware of the deadly, odorless gases that could slowly sneak up on them. If they left too soon, they weren't very productive. If they left too late, they got killed. After a few too many dead miners, someone realized that if they carried a canary in a cage into the mine, the bird would be knocked out by the gases before the men. If the men paid attention to the signs, they could escape death *and* get their work done. Sounds like teaching sometimes, doesn't it?

Wouldn't it be great if there was a signal that alerted teachers that it's time to move on before the class loses focus? Like a warning alarm for engagement levels. It turns out that tool exists, and you already have a couple of them in your room. It's called the Canary Kid. Here's how it works:

Imagine you are doing an hour-long engineering lab where students build tall towers out of marshmallows and spaghetti sticks. The lab will have three parts:

1. Time to build and measure
2. Time to discuss what worked and didn't work
3. A final time to build and measure

You *could* just give them twenty minutes for each stage, but that timing is arbitrary and wouldn't accommodate the natural rhythm of the class. Everyone's attention won't magically begin and end at the same time, and you'll lose some of the productivity that you might have had if you gave them a little more time. *The experienced teacher will instead watch for the Canary Kid.* This is the kid who starts to lose focus first. Maybe he or she stands up and walks around, starts to poke a neighbor, pulls a toy out of his or her pocket, or asks to go get a drink. Whatever off-task behavior the Canary Kid presents, he or she is showing you that the group's attention is starting to wane. *Get ready to switch gears!*

Sometimes Canary Kids lose interest way too fast, and you'll reengage them with some magic words or a specific task to do while they wait. Other times, you may wait for two or three Canary Kids to show themselves before moving on. Once you get good at reading Canary Kids, you'll enjoy smooth transitions, and you won't find yourself facing an entire class of off-task students ever again!

Pro tip: There are Canary Kids among the teachers, too. In the next staff meeting, see who starts to lose focus first. If you are leading the meeting, you can manage your transitions off them. If you can't spot the Canary Kid in that group, it's probably you!

QUICK TRANSITIONS: MOVE TO THE FLOOR!

Sometimes you need a transition *before* the Canary Kid signals. Maybe you are running out of time, the group is taking too long to finish the first stage, or you need to clarify instructions. For a quick transition, take a play from your kindergarten teacher's playbook: *have the group join you on the floor.* (I usually use a chair for myself so kids can see me better and my knees don't explode.)

Moving the whole body and changing the physical environment are both clear signals to focus everyone's attention. Moving to the floor also minimizes distractions. It provides a clear break from the work area so you aren't competing with lab supplies for student attention.

You can also use this hack as a "pause button" in the lab. When you move everyone to the floor to discuss, they leave all the supplies and materials in place. After the discussion is complete, students move right back to what they were doing.

In the example of marshmallows and spaghetti-stick construction, that middle stage of discussion would be a great time for moving to the floor. Kids are separated from the supplies temporarily, and they are better able to join the discussion. When it's over, the movement back to the tables is also a nice transition.

If your space doesn't have room to move everyone to the floor, have them stay in the same spot but change their body position to face a different direction. Just walk to the other side of the room and tell everybody to spin their chair to face you. Even that small movement can help refocus their attention.

Empower the Know-It-All

Everyone loves to feel smart. Kids like to show off what they know, and parents like to hear their child is getting smarter. It seems like kids would be quick to talk about what they learned when they get home, but when parents ask what they did at school, students universally offer one of the following:

1. A shoulder shrug
2. A mumbled "I don't know"
3. A mildly annoyed "nothing"

It's enough to make the teachers drink more than usual.

Support teacher sobriety by bridging the communication gap *and* sneaking in a content review. The trick is to put the words right into their mouths. Here is how it works. At the end of the lab, give the kids a little sermon like this:

> When you get home today, your family is probably going to ask you what you did in class. I know that normally the correct answer is "I don't know" or "nothing." But today is different. Today you have something to tell them about, and you really ought to show them how smart you are! When they ask what you did today, tell them you learned…(insert concept you want kids to remember). *Your parents will be impressed with how smart you are, and you can feel proud that you know more about that subject than anybody in your house!*

Students usually listen pretty closely to that speech, because it gives them license to show off at home. Hopefully the message travels all the way home, and they actually tell it to an adult who asks. But even if they don't, your little content-review sermon will stick in their heads, and they will have that information for the long term.

Quick Cleaning Hacks

Science Club is a wonderful place, but if you're doing it right, you will end up with big messes. You *could* spend forty-five minutes cleaning up after the students leave, *or* you could use these two hacks to quickly put the lab in order at the end of class.

Sneaky Praise

When the group is cleaning up at the end of a meeting, members sometimes lose focus and start to visit with each other. Refocus the group by loudly praising one of the members who *is* cleaning. Use this line: "Brye is doing a great job picking trash up off the floor! Great job, Brye. Grab your bag and get in line!"

Most kids will drop to the floor in an effort to pick up scraps. Follow with: "Lacy is doing a great job cleaning, too! Lacy, go ahead and line up!"

At that point, most kids will be scrambling to clean up, and you can just keep on dismissing the top performers to the line. The remaining kids will work faster and faster until the room is clean.

Litter Ticket

An alternative to sneaky praise is to have kids show you their litter ticket at the door as they leave. Their ticket to leave is the mess they'll retrieve from the floor. Use this line: "Great job, everyone. It's time to go! Your ticket out the door is six pieces of trash! I'll be at the door with the trash can to take your tickets!"

Twenty-five kids times 6 scraps each equals 150 scraps that you don't have to pick up! Just watch out for the smart kids who pick up 1 scrap and tear it into 6 pieces. If they are in your science club, they'll be smart enough for such trickery.

MARCHING THE TROOPS

Moving your group from one room to another is tricky! Kids who have been seated for hours relish the chance to go for a walk with their friends. Activity and noise levels can climb fast. Of course, that excitement happens in the hall where all the other teachers will witness your roving riot.

These two hacks are *great* for maintaining a line without having to tell students anything. They work with students you don't know, and they don't require you to talk (or the kids to listen).

The first hack reduces noise in the line, and the second hack gets your students back into one line when they clump up into groups.

CRAWL THE LINE

Here's how to reduce the chatter and noise in your line so it doesn't get too loud in the hall. *As you lead your line, keep moving.* Don't stop your forward motion. Students in a moving line have to devote attention to keeping their spot in line. Students who like to turn backward to visit will have to focus more on adjusting course instead. If they miss the cue that there is a gap in the line, friends will tell them to move up, or they will attempt to pass them by. Either of these will refocus the slowpokes.

At the places where you normally stop completely, slow down to a crawl that barely creeps along at a single step every few seconds. Even if you are jammed up in a crowd heading for a pep rally, taking a single step will cause a ripple of movement through your line that keeps everyone on their toes.

You can use the same trick if the whole class has to stop in one place as they would for a restroom break, or the PE coach isn't quite finished with the class before yours. Just tell the first person in line to lead the line to the end of the hall and back. You can watch the line the whole time, and the students will be much less fidgety than if they were standing still staring at you for five minutes!

HUG THE CORNERS

Sometimes a line of students slowly clumps up as students move up to walk side by side with a friend. These lumps of talkers make it difficult to move smoothly down the hall, and students walking in blobs are louder than they are when walking in a sleek, straight line. You *could* shout down the hall for everybody to get back in line, but that's not cool, and it's fifty-fifty on whether or not the clump will "hear" you. Sometimes the more energetic kids might even argue with you about it.

Instead of huffing and puffing or having a battle of wits, iron out the lumps easily by hugging the corners. Next time you have a clumping problem, try it out. At the next corner your class comes to, you pause at the corner while the line leader continues leading the line past you. As the line passes between you and the corner, gently move your body closer to the wall, until there is only enough space for one student at a time to pass through. As the clumps approach, the students will have to reform into a line, or crash into you. (I haven't gotten whacked yet.)

Every once in a while, some kids might try to walk behind me to maintain their clump. I just use my arms like an usher directing a crowd to indicate which way to go, and they'll nearly always fall in line.

Because this hack is nonverbal, there's nothing for students to argue with. If you do it with a smile, they might feel helpful guidance rather than bossy redirection.

Pro tip: You can use this trick in a straight run of a hallway too! It is just easier at a corner because the kids are already changing direction. You are just using your body to fine-tune that direction.

PART THE CROWD

Sometimes you'll find yourself walking through a hallway of crowded chaos. (Think passing period at the middle school.) Pushing through that crowd with or without your line of students can be slow and plodding. There is a way to part the herd, though, and to make your way right through the middle without breaking stride. *The trick is in where you point your eyes.*

If you make eye contact with every kid you come to, you'll be bogged down, blocked, and waiting for kids to get out of your way. Instead, fix your gaze slightly above the crowd as if you were looking at somebody at the far end of the hall, and then start walking forward toward that imaginary person. The kids walking at you will magically shift stride to give you your path.

I part crowds that way at the elementary, middle, and high school levels, and it works so well I use it at the mall.

You can also use the direction of your gaze to "red light and green light" other people. People generally assume that you will walk whichever way you are looking. If you have ever approached a single person in an empty hallway and then ended up dancing left and right with him or her, trying to decide which way to pass, you can stop the dancing by looking to the left. He or she will move to your right automagically. (It doesn't matter which direction you choose to look, just that you hold the gaze in that direction until the person passes you.)

QUIET THE CROWD WITH BROKEN SENTENCES

Kids are loud. The first challenge every teacher faces is figuring out how to quiet the noise so he or she can teach. Strategy number one from the new-teacher toolbox is brute force. "Everybody be quiet and listen up!" It *might* work for a little while, but kids get numb to that pretty fast, usually with indignation.

After brute force stops working, it's time for strategy number two: Teacher becomes passive. When the class gets loud, the teacher puts his or her hand up in the air and waits for the second-grade square dancers to sit back down. That can take a while, and the teacher will end up frustrated because the kids have been left in charge.

I used to alternate between strategy one and strategy two, constantly trading control and irritation with the kids. I didn't have much choice until my friend Ms. Barbee taught me a little teacher jujitsu. Under her guidance, I learned how to gather the attention of a loud class without demanding that students surrender control and without waiting for them to give control over like a generous gift. She used a trick I call "Break the Sentence," and it works like this.

Whenever you have a talkative group, instead of telling them to be quiet so you can begin the lesson, just go ahead and begin the lesson. Start talking right into the crowd, just as if they were listening like perfect angels. Don't even give them "the look." Just start your spiel. Some portion of the class may start listening right away, but there will be some who just keep on blabbing. To help them focus, you break the sentence by stopping what you were saying abruptly, right in the middle of the sentence. For example: "Today we are going to be learning about leaves and how they…" (abrupt pause and a silent wait). As soon as there is a minor break in their conversation, begin talking again "…use sunlight to make their own food." If they resume their conversation, break your sentence again.

I like to go stand right next to the talkers to make myself obvious. I have also found it is more effective to pause midsentence than to finish my thought and pause at the period. Usually the first kids to get quiet will end up shushing their friends so that they can hear. You may have to break your sentence a few times to get everybody on the same page, but by pausing during their interruptions, you send a message of calm control rather than the extremes of drill sergeant or wimpy weakling.

Moving to DEFCON 1. Every once in a while you may need to drop the hammer. Maybe you need attention quickly, or the class needs more kindergarten cops than Gandhi. When you have a couple of student holdouts who can't get it together, you can apply Ms. Barbee's full-court press. When she reached her limit of student interruptions, she would break her sentence with the verbal rattlesnake rattle *"I'll wait..."* Then she would pull out the teacher look (you know, chin down, neutral face, looking out from under your eyebrows). After it was quiet, she would pause silently for six full seconds, which seemed like eternity when she was using the look. After it was clear she meant business, she would release the offenders from the death ray with a quiet "Are y'all ready?" Her technique didn't provide openings for argument, and kids didn't mess with Ms. Barbee. With no power struggles, she became everyone's favorite teacher in short order.

*Pro ti*p: "Break the Sentence" is especially useful if you are speaking to a group of loud adults you don't want to offend by shushing them. If you just start and break your sentence a few times, it'll seem as if you are calmly working your way into the presentation instead of being aggressive or disrespectful. I don't suggest the death ray during staff meetings, though. Somebody in the crowd might death ray you right back.

CHAPTER 7

Ten Great Labs to Get You Started!

● ● ●

YOU MAY ALREADY HAVE A few labs you love, but to get you started, here are ten tried and true labs that kids love in Science Club. Each one is designed to encourage student engagement while helping you enjoy the learning process. If you ever need help or have suggestions to improve the labs, connect with me on Twitter @TheFort_FW. I *love* connecting with other teachers, and I can't wait to hear how you're doing! When you get underway, remember to take pictures and post them to show everyone what you're up to in your lab. When you post pictures, remember to tag your school district, your superintendent, and me.

A bucket of mealworms ready for Science Club!

Discover Entomology with Mealworms

● ● ●

NEED HELP WITH THIS LAB? *Ask me*! Find me on Twitter: @ TheFort_FW. Remember to tag your photos with #TSCHB so we can see what's going on in your lab!

Caution: It's common for kids to be unnerved with live bugs. We are taught that bugs are gross, after all. But some people have uncontrollable fear and unreasonable panic triggered by bugs. *These people are rare.* In my experience, they occur about one person per twenty classes. If you *do* encounter a kid who panics at the thought, don't force the activity on him or her. Don't try to "fix" that student or convince him or her that bugs are cool. Give the student the bug books to look through, or deputize him or her as a tool manager.

BACKGROUND

Mealworms are not actually worms. Instead, they are baby beetles (larvae). Worms don't have legs. Impress students by explaining that Earth could be considered Planet of the Beetles and that humans don't even come close to having the same number of individuals. One-fourth of all living creatures on Earth are beetles.

Here's another way to look at it: if you took every animal on Earth, from a tiny little flea up to a big blue whale and put them into a single-file line, every fourth animal would be a beetle. Beetles come in all shapes and sizes, and they include ladybugs and June bugs.

MATERIALS

Get live mealworms from the pet store. Four per child will be plenty. Don't get super/giant worms. They have been treated with hormones to make them big and fat, and they will never morph into beetles. That's why super mealworms generally aren't kept in the fridge. If you aren't sure what to get, just tell them you want small mealworms. I like foil catering trays to use as pans, but paper plates are fine. Condiment containers from the big-box store are cheap and very effective. They're usually next to the paper plates. Mealworms aren't picky and like apples, potatoes, and squash.

* Live mealworms
* Plastic spoons
* Hand lenses
* Pans to observe in
* Oatmeal—the cheap stuff, not flavored
* Plastic containers with lids for habitats
* A thumbtack or sharp pencil for poking holes in the lids
* A potato, apple, or squash that you'll dice into cubes

I also like to bring a few related books to my labs. They are helpful visuals, and if a student has a phobia of live bugs, he or she can check out the books during the lab.

- Every kid remembers reading *The Very Hungry Caterpillar* by Eric Carle in kindergarten, and it makes explaining the life cycle easier. It's in your school library.
- *Mealworms* by Donna Schaffer has great illustrations, and the information is clear and interesting.
- Any beetle or bug books you want to check out from your school library would be helpful.

Suggested Timing for One-Hour Lab

This is a framework; adjust as needed.

- Ten minutes: arrival and show-and-tell
- Ten minutes: introduction meeting—tools, background information, using our senses, expectations, and oatmeal
- Fifteen minutes: mealworm exploration in small groups (if interest is shown for longer, *extend this time*)
- Ten minutes (on the floor): lecture of mealworm life cycle, instars (see the Interesting Facts section), and how to build a mealworm habitat
- Ten minutes: habitat building (can be done in five minutes if they work quickly)
- Five minutes cleanup: (*all* oatmeal swept up, trays stacked, tools gathered and packed, and tables wiped)

Behavior Expectations

- Students should help other students around them feel comfortable. Use specimens for science, not for scaring people.

* These are specimens for learning science, so we will learn from them, not treat them like toys.
* Use the right tool for the right job: hand lenses for looking and spoons and fingers for touching.
* Keep your area neat. Don't make a mess just for entertainment.

Concepts

* Animals have a life cycle that can be observed.
* Insect life cycles have unique stages that can be observed and recorded as they go through METAMORPHOSIS.
* Habitats have different components that work together to support life. Changes within the habitat can help animals thrive, become ill, or die.
* Energy flows from the Sun to the plants (oats) and then to the mealworm that eats it.

Procedure
Prep
Take your pans and put in a handful or two of oatmeal and then sprinkle in five to ten live mealworms in each pan (more is fine). It's OK to stack the pans with the mealworms in them—they don't need much room. If you do this a month in advance, you can have pupae and beetles, too, but the lab works great with just mealworms.

Slice up the pieces of potato for the habitats you are about to build (cubes of about 1 cm work great).

OPENING

Have students meet together on the floor. Explain the day's topic. You will nearly *always* get asked the following three questions:

1. Are they real? (Yes)
2. Are they alive? (Yes)
3. Do we touch them? (Yes. Be gentle, and hold them over the pan.)

Explain the background information for the mealworms, and show students what the mealworms look like (use a book, a projector, or the live specimens).

Demonstrate the tools that students will be using (hand lens and spoons).

If time allows, explain how they will use their senses for investigating mealworms. (If time is short, skip the senses.)

* *Sight.* Students will watch and observe the mealworms.
* *Hearing.* They will listen to background info from teacher.
* *Smell.* They can sniff the mealworms if the students want to. They smell like feet.
* *Touch.* Students can hold the mealworms gently over the pan.
* *Taste.* Mealworms are edible, but we will not taste during this activity because some kids are unknowingly allergic to eating mealworms. Also, these mealworms have probably been handled before.

Show students what the mealworms will look like as adult beetles. They are called darkling beetles. All beetles are insects. Generally, insects are recognized easily because they have:

- Six legs
- Three body sections (head, abdomen, and thorax)
- Four wings
- Antennae on their heads

Yes, ants do have four wings. Remember the queen. Finally, explain about the oatmeal. Mealworms love oatmeal for three reasons:

1. They eat it.
2. They get their water from it.
3. They live inside it. (I usually have the kids imagine what it would be like to live inside of a house made out of their favorite food.)

Note. Some kids misunderstand and think that their oatmeal at home has bugs in it. Reassure them that regular oatmeal doesn't have bugs in it, but if they ever end up with a mealworm for a pet, they'll know just what to feed it.

Have the kids move to the tables to work in groups of two or three. Pass out the mealworms and tools, and let them begin their investigations. As the kids play and observe, circulate through the room validating observations and asking guiding questions. This activity is a free-exploration time that can be as short as ten minutes or as long as time or the Canary Kid allows. If the kids are too timid to touch the specimens, model the action by walking over to a group and asking, "Have you touched one yet?" Do this while showing how to touch the mealworm, and the kids will follow your lead. As the end of the observation time approaches, give students a two-minute warning.

Move back to the floor *or* clear the pans off the tables temporarily to teach the life cycle of the mealworm. (Don't try to teach kids who have bugs in front of them—it won't happen.) Explain the four stages (egg, larva, pupa, and adult darkling beetle) of the mealworm life cycle. Explain the term metamorphosis. Now is a good time to explain the similarities between the mealworm life cycle and the butterfly life cycle using Eric Carle's book *The Very Hungry Caterpillar* because nearly every student has read it. It's not necessary to read the whole book to them. Kids will be interested to learn that to enter the pupa stage, the larva's body dissolves to goo and then reforms into the shape of the beetle. As the beetles mature, they lay their eggs, and one beetle can lay up to 250 eggs!

Building Habitats

Mealworms make great pets because they don't bark, tear up the couch, steal your food, or make a mess on the floor. Put their habitat safely on a shelf or in a drawer, and they'll happily go through their life cycle. Teaching kids how to build a mealworm habitat using the three-two-one strategy is easy, and it simplifies the process.

* Three mealworms
* Two spoons of oatmeal
* One piece of squash/potato/apple

Students will put these components into their container, and snap the lid on. They can use a thumbtack or a pencil to poke a hole in the lid of their habitat. If they see water droplets form inside the container, they need to make more holes, or their oatmeal will get moldy, and the mealworms will die.

The mealworms won't need extra water. They will die if more is added. They get all the hydration they need from the oatmeal and squash/potato. It's also a nice place to lay their eggs.

Common Concerns

Kids often worry that their mealworms will run out of food and water or that they'll crawl out of the holes in the lid. Tell them not to worry. Two spoons of oatmeal will feed and water them for their whole lifetime, and mealworms aren't adventurous enough to crawl away from their food. The holes shouldn't be big enough, anyway.

It's fine if the mealworms get buried in the oatmeal. They like that sort of thing. Don't worry if they are just lying there. They can be kind of lazy.

Conclusion

Return to the tables or pass out the pans. Give the students containers and make habitats. Having a couple of pans of just oatmeal set around the tables makes the process faster if time is short.

Have students clean up any spilled oatmeal and then move to the floor for the wrap-up discussion.

Kids usually want to know what to do with their specimens. They have several options:

* They can let the beetles stay in their container until they die of old age.
* They can upgrade to a larger container to start a mealworm colony.

* They can give them to their science teacher or a friend who is interested.
* They can feed the mealworms to a reptile, bird, or rodent.
* They can freeze them and add them to a bug collection.
* They can establish a colony to clean skeletons like museums do (see below).
* Only the brave will research mealworm recipes to whip up a snack.

Note. Students shouldn't release mealworms or beetles into the local environment because of the potential impact they could have.

BONUS

When you are done with the activity, do yourself a favor and give yourself a mealworm colony. Just pour the remnants into an aquarium, a plastic shoe box, or a two-liter soda bottle with holes to create your own classroom colony. Mealworms are *very* low maintenance. You can ignore them for months, and they'll be fine. There are only three things that I've seen kill a colony:

* if the school sprays for bugs, and you leave them in the room during the spray;
* moldy oatmeal from too much water; and
* excessive heat from being left in a parked car (hot classrooms in summer are fine).

You will have constant access to an active life cycle and metamorphosis example, your students will be impressed with your amazing science skills, parents and administrators will be impressed with how deeply you engage with the content, and you will be impressed with how little you have to do to keep the thing going (maybe you add a handful of oatmeal next year. Or maybe you don't.)

INTERESTING FACTS

Mealworms are not worms. Mealworms have legs, and true worms do not. Mealworms won't "grow back" if they are split in half. (Neither will most earthworms.)

Mealworms shed or molt their skin/exoskeleton regularly. When mealworms molt, they appear white, but then their skin darkens to the orange-and-brown color. If you need a little more excitement in your lab, you can sneak a quick poof of air into the pans to make the skins "leap" into the air. It only works if your mealworms have been living and shedding in that pan for a few weeks, *and* if you can handle the shrieks of startled entomologists.

A mealworm's age is measured in INSTARS. Their age isn't tied to the passage of time as much as a person's age is. Their development is more affected by how warm or cool their environment is and how plentiful the resources are in their environment. That's why when you buy mealworms at the pet store, they come out of the fridge. They are chilled to keep them in suspended animation so that they don't turn into beetles. Every time a mealworm sheds its exoskeleton, it's called an instar. When students ask how long it takes a mealworm to change into a beetle, it takes about ten to twelve instars. Those instars may take one to two months or much longer if the mealworms are kept in the fridge.

Students are often curious about whether their specimen is a boy or a girl. The only technique I have heard of is to take the mealworm and flip it belly up. On the seventh body segment (from the head), a female will have two white spots, and a male will have nothing. Although my students have claimed success with that technique, I've never had luck with it.

Beetles have been used for years to clean meat off skeletons in museum collections. Their skills as decomposers help them to strip away the soft tissue, leaving behind the bones. They'll usually even leave the ligaments and tendons alone, so the skeletons stay connected. In museums, dermestid beetles are used because they work quickly, but mealworms and darkling beetles can easily do the same work. I have seen the cleaning firsthand, thanks to the occasional uninvited gecko creeping through my classroom. Predictably, the sight of three hundred wiggling mealworms will sometimes tempt a gecko to jump into the tank. If they aren't noticed and rescued, they'll die in the tank. Imagine my surprise the first time I found a cleaned gecko skeleton lying in my mealworm colony! I now keep an eye out for small specimens that have died (grass snake, lizard, or small turtle), and I add them to my mealworm tank. A month later, I have bones!

Mealworms are edible. They have lots of protein and are a much more efficient and sustainable food source than beef or pork. Sometimes they're flavored like potato chips, but they can also be included in stir-fry, baked goods, or dipped in chocolate. Many cultures eat insects, and it's likely that insects will become more accepted into cultures that didn't initially embrace them. Remember when nobody knew what sushi was? Now you can buy it at the grocery store. Watch out for mealworms in the deli case!

Beetles are ARTHROPODS. *Arthr* means "joint," and *pod* means "leg or foot." Beetles have jointed legs, and they fall into the arthropod group with all other insects, crustaceans, and spiders. Explain that to be an arthropod, you need jointed legs, *and* an exoskeleton. Humans have leg joints, but our bones are inside, so we are not arthropods.

Beetles have no bones. Instead, they have an EXOSKELETON. It is the outer shell or covering that protects their bodies. Help students remember the prefix *ex* means "outside or away from" by having them blow on their hand (exhale) and looking at the sign leading out of the building (exit).

Analyze Arthropods through Crayfish Dissection

● ● ●

NEED HELP WITH THIS LAB? *Ask me*! Find me on Twitter: @ TheFort_FW. Remember to tag your photos with #TSCHB so we can see what's going on in your lab! This lab is a great introduction to dissection. Students get the wow factor of dissection without sharp tools or lots of technical knowledge.

Caution: People with a shellfish allergy should not handle crayfish. If they are allergic to shrimp, they will be allergic to crayfish, too. (It's actually the iodine in the shellfish that folks are allergic to.)

BACKGROUND

Crayfish have lots of aliases. They are known as crayfish, crawfish, crawdads, mudbugs, écrevisse (from French), and sometimes even mini-lobsters. (They aren't really lobsters.) They are common in freshwater streams and creeks, and chances are that you are less than a mile from some wild crayfish right now. They are OMNI-VORES, and they will eat just about anything including grasses, other plants, dead animals, live animals, and even cardboard. They are also DECOMPOSERS (detritivores), and they are a popular meal for folks who don't mind eating bug butts for dinner.

Crayfish have no bones. Their protection and support structure comes instead from an EXOSKELETON. The prefix *ex* means "outside or away from." To help kids remember the prefix *ex*, have kids push their air out of their body (EXhale) and point to the sign that marks the way out of the building (EXit). The exoskeleton provides a shell of protection for the crayfish, but it doesn't grow. As the animal grows larger, it will need to shed/molt its exoskeleton periodically and grow another one (like a kid getting rid of shoes that don't fit anymore). Crayfish have no neck, so they can't turn their heads to see danger sneaking up behind them. Luckily, they can push their eyes out away from their head on EYE STALKS. This lets them see backward and all around for protection.

Crayfish have no lungs, but rather they breathe with gills located under the largest section of their exoskeleton called the CARAPACE. It protects the head, gills, and most of the digestive system. Their large claws are called CHELIPEDS, and they use them for defense, for tearing off bites of food to eat, and for fighting. If they lose a cheliped in battle, they can regrow another one. They also use their strong tail muscles to rocket them backward in the water if they sense danger. They just take their tail and slap it hard toward their belly, and they shoot backward to safety.

Crayfish are DECAPODS. *Deca* means "ten," and *pod* means "leg or foot." To help kids remember the prefix *deca*, remind them that a decade is ten years. To count all ten legs, you *do* include the large claw/chelipeds, and the other eight walking legs, but you *don't* include the soft, floppy swimmerets along their abdomen/tail. Those swimmerets help move water over the eggs that the females will carry on their abdomen so that they get enough oxygen. Sometimes crayfish will be missing legs from fights or predators, but you can still count the stumps.

Fun fact. December used to be the tenth month on the calendar. In 713 BC, Numa Pompilius (king of Rome) added January and February to the beginning of the year, and it threw the calendar names off.

How can you tell the males from the females? It's easy. *Just watch them carefully and see which bathroom they walk into.* In reality, you flip them onto their back, and look where the tail meets the carapace. The males will have two hard swimmerets behind (posterior to) their walking legs and in front of (anterior to) their soft swimmerets. These are sperm depositors used for reproduction. The females will be lacking the two hard swimmerets and will instead have a small opening in the same spot to receive sperm from the males. (It usually looks like a white dot.)

Crayfish are also arthropods. *Arthr-* means "joint," and *pod* means "leg or foot." To help students remember the prefix *arthr-*, remind them of their grandmother's aching joints. Arthritis is what gives her pain. *-Itis* is a suffix that means "pain or inflammation." Arthropods make up over 80 percent of all living species (on Earth, that is). Arthropods all have exoskeletons, jointed legs, and segmented bodies. They range in size from microscopic to the Japanese spider crab that can spread its claws to a span of twelve feet.

Crayfish are great at digging and burrowing through mud. Tunneling gives them a place to hibernate during fall and winter, and it also helps to aerate soils that they dig through. Burrows can be up to three or four feet deep, and they are usually filled with water. As crayfish scoop out the mud from their tunnel, they will use their claws and mouth to form the mud into mud balls and then use the mud balls like bricks to build a chimney at the mouth of the burrow. The chimney might be a strategy for increasing airflow in the tunnel, and if a drought comes, the crayfish might seal up the chimney to keep the moisture in.

There are over three hundred types of crayfish that live in North America, and sometimes they are raised as a farm crop to be an income source or a food source. The warm, wet climate in Louisiana and east Texas is great for raising crayfish, although there are plenty of other places where crayfish farming is possible. Rice farmers often raise crayfish as a second crop because the growing conditions for rice and crayfish are similar, and their harvest seasons occur at different times. The stubble and plant pieces left behind after the rice harvest are eaten by the crayfish as they grow, and the crayfish burrows help aerate the mud for better rice crops.

MATERIALS
See "Finding Crayfish for Science Club" at the end of this section for further notes on crayfish.

* Crayfish—one or two per pair of students
* Plastic spoons
* Hand lenses
* Baby wipes
* Pans/trays
* Table wipes

SUGGESTED TIMING FOR ONE-HOUR LAB
This is a framework; adjust as needed.

* Ten minutes: arrival and show-and-tell
* Ten minutes: introduction meeting—background information, external structures, tools, and expectations

- Fifteen minutes: exploration/observation in small groups (if interest is shown for longer, *extend this time*)
- Ten minutes (on the floor): life cycle, farming, habitat, gender, and how to open/dissect
- Ten minutes: dissection (look for gills, brain, heart, and stomach)
- Five minutes: cleanup (*all* scraps in the trash, trays and tools cleaned and dried, and tables wiped)

BEHAVIOR EXPECTATIONS

- Students will help other students around them feel comfortable. Use specimens for science, not for scaring people.
- Specimens are for learning science. We will learn from them, not treat them like toys.
- Use the right tool for the job: hand lenses are for looking, not scooping.
- Keep your area neat. Don't make a mess just for entertainment.

CONCEPT

Crayfish have unique structures with functions that help them thrive in their natural environment.

2 scientists investigate shrimp in Decapod Dissection class.
Shrimp are a great substitute when crayfish are out of season!

Procedure

Begin with a meeting to provide background information about crayfish (on the floor or at desks). Explain habitats, tools students will be using, and student expectations and then explain the first four body parts that you would like students to find:

- Rostrum. The unicorn spike on a crayfish's forehead that makes it look angry. This spike helps protect the face.
- Telson. Spread the tail fan open. The middle part of the fan is the telson. On the bottom of the telson is where waste leaves the body.
- Eye stalks. Crayfish can push their eyes out from their heads on eye stalks. This lets them have a larger field of vision.
- Chelipeds. The large claws on the front two legs of the crayfish.

Release students to their seats, and pass out specimens and tools (one crayfish per pair of students increases engagement). As students examine their specimen, move around the room asking guiding questions and answering student requests. The experiences in this portion of the lab are the most valuable, so if their interest holds, let them go longer than you had planned.

Pro tip: If you have a class that is reluctant to touch the specimens, ask them if they have ever felt a crayfish before *while you reach over and feel it.* When you finally see a student touch a crayfish, ask him or her what it felt like. When the student answers, his or her friends will want to confirm by touching the crayfish as well. This modeling of how to touch the crayfish will be more effective than just telling the student to touch it.

When it's time to transition to the next portion, instruct each group to count how many legs their specimen has, and when they have their number, move back to the floor. When everyone is back to the floor, discuss the terms DECAPOD and ARTHROPOD. Explain how the crayfish uses its EXOSKELETON for protection. (These terms are explained within the background information.)

Before moving to dissection, explain to the group what the lab conclusion and cleanup will look like. All the specimen parts will go in the trash, tools will be washed, dried, and stored, and table tops will be wiped down. Students shouldn't keep parts of the specimen (they will ask) because specimens will quickly decompose and smell terrible.

Model how to dissect the crayfish. To open the crayfish, you don't need knives or any other tools. Instead, you need to imagine lifting the pull tab on a can of soda to open it. This is the same action for opening a crayfish. Simply put your fingernail under the back edge of the carapace and lift it up and off. (The carapace is the largest section of the exoskeleton.) If you want to impress the group, have them be really quiet so that they can hear the science noises created by the lifting of the carapace.

Show them the structures they'll be looking for:

- GILLS. These are the feathery-looking structures on the sides once the carapace is lifted off. They are usually white or gray.
- BRAIN. This is the grayish blob that is right behind the eyeballs, inside the carapace. Some will be easier to see than others because it depends on how the carapace is lifted.
- HEPATOPANCREAS. This is the yellow goo (or brownish tan in specimens that aren't fresh). It's a gland that aids in digestion. It does the work that the liver (*hepat*) and the pancreas do in humans. This goo is also called mustard, tomalley, or crab fat, and it is considered a delicacy. It is not poop.

Release the group back to their tables.

Once they are back at their tables, give them a chance to work their way into the carapace. Rotate through the groups to monitor progress and behavior. If you see conduct that needs redirection, the easiest way to manage it is to pick up that group's whole tray and walk away. After thirty seconds, walk back, reinforce what you'd like to see, and then return their supplies.

Pro tip: If a student claims to feel ill or too grossed out to continue, look for his or her smile. If the student is legitimately feeling overwhelmed, let him or her sit and rest by the door or go get a drink of water. If the student is being dramatic for fun, offer to set the trash can by his or her chair so that he or she can barf into it as the student works. After thousands of crayfish dissections, I've never seen barf in the trash can with this strategy.

Wrap up with cleaning the lab space, discarding leftovers, and having final discussion as time allows. The baby wipes are *great* for hands, tables, and pans. Make sure to take out the trash—dead crawfish are not forgiving.

Interesting Facts

You can catch crayfish by tying a piece of meat on a string (chicken legs work great), tossing it into a stream, and waiting. After letting it sit awhile, slowly pull it in, and be ready to put your net under the chicken leg when you lift it out of the water. Another strategy is to take your net and rub catfish stink bait on the inside of the net and put it into the water. Let it sit awhile, and then pull the net out with the crayfish already inside.

The name *crayfish* probably came from English speakers trying to pronounce the French word *écrevisse*. French culture was (and is) strong around New Orleans and the rest of Louisiana, and crayfish can often be found in the food there.

There are over five hundred species of crayfish, and they live all over the world. Some adult crayfish can be as small as three centimeters long, and some species can weigh as much as eight pounds.

A mother crayfish carries her eggs on her abdomen, and after they hatch, she carries the babies for up to twenty weeks until they are mature enough to take care of themselves.

A crayfish can lay over 450 eggs at a time.

When males are ready to mate, they shed/molt their juvenile exoskeleton and grow a thicker and stronger exoskeleton with bigger claws, sharper spines, and a longer body. This new and improved "battle body" helps them fight other males more effectively to win a female. When mating season is over, they molt, and they look like juveniles again.

Crayfish legs have a breaking point that easily snaps off if they are grabbed or attacked. This lets them escape, leaving part of their leg behind. When this occurs, they just regrow the missing leg.

When crayfish molt, their body is soft until their new exoskeleton hardens. During that time, they have to watch out for their neighbors, because crayfish are cannibals if they find an unprotected crayfish.

Crayfish (and other arthropods) do not have red blood like the blood that animals with backbones have. Instead, they have hemolymph. Instead of being red with iron like human blood, it is greenish-blue with copper. When the animal dies, and the hemolymph stops receiving oxygen, it quickly turns gray.

Finding Crayfish for Science Club

The best way to get crayfish for your science club is to purchase specimens from a grocery store or fish market. *They will be alive.* Crayfish are generally only available in spring because of farming cycles in Louisiana. They are sometimes available in the off season from Asian markets that import them.

Take a cooler to pick them up. You will only need three or four pounds for a meeting (that may even be overkill). Crayfish are usually killed quickly by boiling for dinner, but for Science Club, it will be better to put them into the freezer. Their systems will slow gently to a stop and will remain intact for dissection. If your crayfish package from the store is too unwieldy to put directly into the freezer, use cooking tongs or a fifth grader to move them into Ziploc bags or plastic containers for freezing.

The alternative to buying and freezing is to purchase preserved specimens from a science supplier. Preserved specimens are much more expensive than live crayfish, and you'll need to plan for handling the chemicals and disposal required when you are finished. The preserved specimens always smell worse, too.

If you can't find crayfish anywhere, switch to whole shrimp with the heads still on. If you are ever at the store, and you see that crayfish are in season, consider purchasing a few for later use. They'll keep for a long time in the freezer.

Note. Crayfish that have been frozen whole aren't food anymore. They are strictly for your science club after that.

Earthworm Exploration

• • •

Need help with this lab? *Ask me!* Find me on Twitter: @ TheFort_FW. Remember to tag your photos with #TSCHB so we can see what's going on in your lab!

Background

Earthworms are small, tube-shaped animals that live underground. They are also called worm, angleworm, or night crawler. They are from the phylum *Annelida*, and they spend their lives burrowing through soil and eating dirt and the dead plant matter within the dirt. Earthworms breathe through their skin, so they need to stay damp. If they are submerged underwater, though, they drown.

They have no internal or external skeleton or shell. Instead, their protection is to live underground, away from predators. This protection is so effective that for over twenty years, scientists in Idaho thought that the giant Palouse earthworm had gone extinct, until they looked a little harder and realized the worms were there all along. Now they aren't even listed as endangered. How does a three-foot-long worm hide for twenty years?!

There are hundreds of different kinds of earthworms, and they range in size from half an inch long, to over ten feet long!

Earthworms are HERMAPHRODITIC (they are both boys *and* girls). Some earthworms find a mate to reproduce with, and others use PARTHENOGENESIS (one overly efficient worm fertilizing itself). Earthworms produce egg capsules that are deposited in their burrows.

Earthworms are a useful tool for gardeners, because they loosen the soil as they burrow, and they also pull nutrients on the surface into the ground.

Earthworms don't have eyes, but they can still see light. Their skin has light-detecting cells on it, and the worms usually try to avoid light.

MATERIALS
Need help finding worms? See "Finding Earthworms for Science Club" at the end of this section.

* Earthworms: one to two per student
* Plastic cups with lids
* Spray bottle with water in it
* Thumbtack for air holes
* One bag of topsoil
* Plastic spoons
* Coffee grounds (can be used grounds)
* Hand lenses
* Trays or pans to hold the worms

SUGGESTED TIMING FOR ONE-HOUR LAB
This is a framework; adjust as needed.

* Ten minutes: arrival and show-and-tell

- Ten minutes (on the floor): introduction meeting on tools, external body parts, using our senses, student expectations, and spray bottle
- Fifteen minutes: worm exploration/observation in small groups (if interest is shown for longer, *extend this time*)
- Ten minutes (on the floor): meeting time on earthworm habitat, gender, and how to build an earthworm habitat
- Ten minutes: habitat building
- Five minutes: cleanup (*all* dirt swept up, trays and tools cleaned and dried, and tables wiped)

Behavior Expectations

- Students will help each other feel comfortable. Specimens are for science, not for scaring people.
- Specimens are for learning science, so we will learn from them, not treat them like toys.
- Use the right tool for the right job: hand lenses for looking and spoons and fingers for touching.
- Keep your area neat. Don't make a mess just for entertainment.

Concepts

- Earthworms are a benefit to the ecology of an environment.
- Decomposers help to clean and purge environments through recycling nutrients.

PROCEDURE

After arrival and opening procedures, gather students together for an introduction meeting. Explain that today we will be learning about earthworms. Give students an overview of earthworm background. (See interesting facts below.) Students will have a chance to examine live specimens *as long as they agree to treat the earthworms nicely.* Explain that in a few minutes, everyone will receive a tray with a live specimen in it, along with a spoon and a hand lens. (Partners are fine if you have limited supplies.) When they receive their specimen, they need to explore the worm and hunt specifically for the following structures:

Clitellum. A ring or saddle-shaped section of the body that stores eggs. The clitellum is closer to the head than the tail, and sometimes it is a lighter color than the rest of the rings.

Setae. The stiff hairs or bristles that give the earthworm traction as it moves through the soil. These anchors prevent backsliding as the worm pushes and pulls through the soil. Setae are usually too small to see but can be felt by touching a live worm. (Dead worms are too relaxed and soft for the students to feel the setae.) Setae are also what makes it difficult to pull a worm out of the ground.

Individual rings/body segments. Earthworms have between 100 and 150 ring-shaped segments. Each muscular ring can expand and contract independently, allowing movement. Their movement (peristaltic motion) consists of pushing the front of the body forward, anchoring the forward end, and then pulling the rear forward.

Remind students that as they explore their earthworm, they will need to be gentle. Earthworms have no bones or exoskeleton to protect them, and the slime on their skin is important because it keeps them moist. They must stay moist because they breathe through their skin. If their skin dries out, they will suffocate! That's why after a big rain, earthworms may crawl safely onto a sidewalk, but then they get stuck and die when the sun comes out.

Release the scientists to explore.

As they examine their earthworms, move around the room making sure students are being gentle. Carry your spray bottle with you, and spray the worms periodically to keep them moist. Don't spray the kids unless you want a loud riot. *Give students as much time at this stage as possible. This exploration time is the point of the whole lab.* If you see students being too rough or using the tools or specimens incorrectly, the most effective way to get them back on track is to quietly walk up, pick up their worm tray, and walk away. They'll know what you mean. After thirty seconds, you can quietly walk back to them and ask, "Are you ready to treat the specimens nicely?" When they say yes (kids always say yes), set it back down and walk away.

After students have had time to explore and examine their specimens, call them back to the floor. (It will be impossible for them to listen if they are still sitting with their earthworms.) Explain how earthworms are a benefit to the environment. They are wonderful to have in your garden because they are:

Decomposers. An earthworm eats leaves, stems, and other bits of plants that have fallen on the ground. Just like little garbage men, they slowly help clean up and digest the dead scraps.

Aerators. As plants grow, they push their roots out farther and farther. If the ground is hard, it's difficult for a plant to push its roots forward. As earthworms tunnel through the soil, they make the ground softer and more fluffy, and the plants have an easier time growing!

Fertilizers. As earthworms eat, their body breaks down the dead plant material into a form that plants can use to grow. Also, earthworms will sometimes eat things off the surface and then go back underground. When they poop, those nutrients are now undergrounds where plants can use them!

CONCLUSION

Remind students that earthworms (and all animals) need food, shelter, and water to survive. Students will be building an earthworm habitat to take home, and they'll need to listen to your instructions for how to build it.

Students will take one of the plastic cups and fill it about three-quarters full of *damp* topsoil. As they add the topsoil, they can gently put their worm in. It doesn't matter if it is at the bottom, middle, or top of the cup. Students will then add a spoonful of coffee grounds to the top of the soil for their earthworm to munch on. After a final dampening of the soil, they will snap the lid on and poke a couple of holes in the lid. After they get their worms home, the students should keep them cool. Earthworms like low temperatures and will do best where it is nice and cool. Students should also monitor the top of their soil. If they see mold starting to form, they should poke a few more holes in the lid to let moisture out faster. Finally, they should watch out for bad smells. Dead earthworms smell terrible. When the habitat starts to stink, it's time to throw it away. You'll probably get a few chuckles when you remind them not to try to revive their worms with CPR.

Note. Some teachers worry about sending earthworms home because parents might get upset. *Don't worry.* After sending earthworms home with over a thousand kids, I have never seen a parent get upset about it. They are usually pleased that their child is

his large shad minnow from the fishing store was a great
tro specimen for Marine Biology. Inexpensive too! He's
about 3 inches long, but you can use bigger if you like.

enjoying real science. Besides, any student living with a worm-hating parent needs creepy-crawly science more than the teacher needs quiet parents.

INTERESTING FACTS

Earthworms are annelids. The Latin root of the word *annelid* is the same as the word *anus*. It means "ring." Earthworms consist of a collection of muscular rings, so it isn't a surprise that their name means "little anus animal."

When students ask if their earthworm is a boy or a girl, just tell them yes! Earthworms have both male and female reproductive structures.

Worm poop, called casting, is so good for your garden that stores sell it as a product. Earthworms usually deposit it onto the surface of the ground. If you find little piles of dirt that look like tiny ant hills with no ants, you have discovered the poop.

Earthworms are edible (called *noke* by chefs in New Zealand). Worms eat lots of dirt, though, so if you decide to cook up some yard spaghetti, you ought to let them live in a dish of cornmeal for a few days to let them poop out the grit before you slurp up your night-crawler noodles. Also, worms from your yard will be full of whatever chemicals have been sprayed on your yard in the last forty years, so munch carefully.

Earthworms are not insects. Worms have no legs, and insects have six.

It's possible for some earthworms to regenerate/regrow a missing head or tail if it is cut off. For this to happen however, the conditions must by very comfortable and supportive for the worm. This lab doesn't foster that sort of regeneration, so if students cut a worm in half, *it will just die*. Some flatworms *can* reproduce by tearing themselves in half, and each half heals to make twins, but earthworms don't reproduce that way.

Earthworms have five hearts. Sometimes their hearts are called aortic arches because they are much less complex than the heart in a mammal.

Earthworms cannot see, but they can detect light. This helps them to avoid crawling onto the surface during the heat of the day when they would dry out too fast. It also helps them avoid places where predators might eat them.

Earthworms don't have teeth for chewing. They use a GIZ-ZARD instead. The gizzard is a section of the stomach that grinds and mushes up their food. When they eat little rocks or sand, those pieces act like little teeth in the gizzard to help grind up their food.

FINDING EARTHWORMS FOR SCIENCE CLUB

The best place to purchase earthworms is from a fishing-supply store. Most big-box retailers that carry fishing supplies will have them. It doesn't matter for this lab what kind you get, but usually bigger is more fun. Make sure they're still alive before you buy them. If they smell rotten, don't get them. Good worms smell either like nothing or like dirt. If you don't have a fishing supplier near you, Amazon.com will deliver live worms to you. They are sometimes called night crawlers or live bait. When you get your earthworms, store them in the fridge until it's time to use them. Bonus points if you store them in the teacher's-lounge fridge.

If your store doesn't carry worms, perhaps you could take up worm fiddling, worm charming, or worm grunting. These are

a collection of techniques used to catch v ground to encourage worms to the surface petitions to see who is the best worm gru get good at it, you could be crowned the W Queen of Sopchoppy, Florida. Really.

Gyotaku Fish Printing

● ● ●

NEED HELP WITH THIS LAB? *Ask me!* Find me on Twitter: @ TheFort_FW. Remember to tag your photos with #TSCHB so we can see what's going on in your lab!

Caution: Fish allergies aren't very common, but they do exist, so be aware.

BACKGROUND

Did you ever notice how diligent fishermen are about taking pictures of everything they catch? Documenting the fish story is an important part of the experience! But what did fishermen do before cameras?

In Japan, fishermen used to travel on long fishing trips, and when they'd catch a good-looking fish, they would need to butcher and preserve it quickly so that it would stay good for the long journey home. When they got home, they had plenty of food and loads of great fishing stories but no evidence of how big their biggest fish had been.

Gyotaku became the solution. In Japanese, *gyo* means "fish" and *taku* means "print." Some intrepid fisherman must have gotten tired of his brother-in-law never believing his fish stories, so he started taking paper and ink with him on his trips. When he'd catch a nice fish, he'd spread ink over one side of the fish and then press it onto the paper to create an image that would last long enough to prove his fishing skills. Eventually, fishermen got so good at making these prints that they started hanging them up as art. A few emperors liked the gyotaku prints so much that they started making special orders of prints that they'd like to hang up in the palace!

MATERIALS

The fish should not be cleaned or gutted, and the scales should not be removed. See "Finding Fish for Science Club" at the end of this section. Manila or construction paper works fine. White printer paper doesn't work because it won't absorb the paint well. The best is art paper for painting with watercolors, but it's expensive. If you use colorful construction paper, use paint colors with high contrast to see the prints clearly. A half sheet of paper will fit most fish.

- Whole fish with scales: one fish per pair or trio of students
- Paper to print on
- Pans or trays to hold fish
- Paper towels
- Paint (tempura works great)
- Colored pencils
- Paper plates or cups to hold paint
- Baby wipes for cleanup

* Hand lenses
* Paintbrushes (smaller works best unless your fish is really big)

Optional Dissection

* Dissection tools (sharp scissors and plastic spoons)
* Completely thawed fish for dissection

Suggested Timing for One-Hour Lab
This is a framework; adjust as needed.

* Ten minutes: arrival and show-and-tell
* Ten minutes: introduction meeting on gyotaku information, fish body parts to look for, and tool orientation
* Ten minutes: explore and observe fish specimens in groups (if interest is shown for longer, *extend this time*)
* Ten minutes: meeting on printing technique, what supplies to use, and where drying area will be
* Fifteen minutes: gyotaku printing time
* Five minutes: cleanup (scraps in the trash, paint wiped up and washed off, and trays and tools cleaned and dried)

Optional Dissection
Dissection won't fit into the one-hour time slot along with the printing, but if you have time, go for it! How often do kids have a chance to dissect a fish? If you want to save time but still hold a

dissection, have the students observe while the teacher dissects a single specimen.

* Ten minutes: orientation about dissection tools and what they'll be looking for
* Fifteen minutes: dissection and then cleanup
* Ten minutes: wrap-up meeting to discuss what they discovered

BEHAVIOR EXPECTATIONS

* Help other students feel comfortable around the specimens.

Preparing a perch for gyotaku printing

- These are specimens for learning science, so we will learn from them, not treat them like toys.
- Use the right tool for the right job: hand lenses for looking, fingers for touching, and brushes for creating.
- Keep your area neat. Don't make a mess just for entertainment.

CONCEPT

Fish have unique body parts that help them to survive in an underwater environment.

PROCEDURE

SETUP

It helps to rinse the fish off before the lab to get rid of the slime layer and any loose scales. If you don't have time, the first couple of prints will do it for you.

Fish can be a little drippy/oozy. Gently pressing them between a couple of paper towels will eliminate most of the ooze before the kids get started. Keep them under damp paper towels when they aren't being used so that the fins don't get crunchy.

Have students meet together on the floor, and introduce the background of the gyotaku process. Explain the history and uses for the technique.

Give behavior expectations, and explain the tools needed for observation:

- Hand lenses are for looking through, not touching things with. Hold them close to the specimen, not up to your eye.

* Spoons are for moving the fish if you don't want to use your fingers. They aren't for jabbing, cutting, or launching fish parts.

As students examine their fish, they will hunt for three body parts. Feel free to change or add to the three parts as needed.

* *Gill cover.* This is the bony cover that protects the gills. It is often confused for the actual gill which is the pinkish red frilly thing *under* the cover.
* *Caudal fin.* This is the tail. It is used as the main thruster to push the fish through the water.
* *Dorsal fin.* This is the fin on the back that sticks out of the water in the shark movies. It helps control direction like the rudder on a boat.

Send students to the table, and pass out fish and tools. Groups of two or three students work great. As they observe, rotate around the room to monitor discussions and to provide clarifications. This observation and exploration period is the most valuable part of the lab, so if their interest holds, consider letting this time go longer. Remind the students to keep their fish in good condition during their exploration because they will need them during the second half of the lab. No fin-breaking or scale-scraping, please!

After the exploration time is over, bring students back to the floor, or pick up their trays so you can explain how to print a fish using gyotaku. Don't try to talk to them if the fish are still in front of them. A fish trumps a teacher for attention every time.

GYOTAKU PRINTING PROCEDURE

Lay your fish on its side in the tray. If it was damaged during the exploration, place the damaged side down and the pretty side up. Make sure that any slime or goo on the surface is wiped away. Take your paintbrush, and cover *one side* (the top side) of the fish from nose to tail with paint. Elementary students should use one color. Older students might want to carefully paint different colors onto different parts of the fish. Paint every nook, crack, and cranny. Everything that you want to appear in your print needs paint on it. The paint needs to be in a thin layer—less is *definitely* better. Just enough to cover the fish like ink on a rubber stamp.

After the side of the fish has paint, take your paper and lay it onto the fish. Use one hand to hold the paper firmly in place, and use the other hand to press it down over the fish. The paper will get pushed all the way down around the fish, making contact with every part of the nose, fins, and tail. The paper will get wrinkly and kind of squashed.

Be careful not to let the paper slip, or your picture will smear. After the paper is pressed all the way down around the fish, carefully lift it straight up and lay it out flat to dry. Usually there will be enough paint still on the fish to make a second print, and often the second print is more detailed than the first one. If there are missing parts within the picture, use a pencil to sketch them in after the paint has dried. Have everyone put their name on their print. It will help if you explain that kids rarely have good results on the first few prints, but after a few tries, they'll get the hang of it.

As students begin their prints, walk around, complementing the shapes and textures that came out well, and model the technique for the students who are having trouble. Have students create a school of fish on their paper if they stop after one or two prints.

Pro tip: Sometimes kids are squeamish about taking their art home. I tell them to take them home. If they don't want them, they can throw them away after they show their parents. They usually like them once they get home.

A good extension activity for the students who finish first is to take the colored pencils and sketch in a background showing the fish's natural habitat.

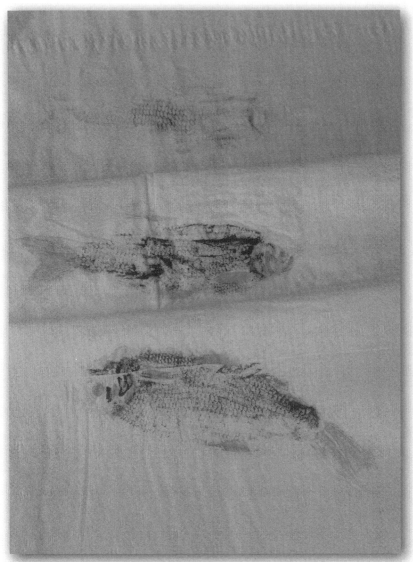

Examples of finished gyotaku on tissue

Conclusion

Have the students wipe down their specimen with a damp paper towel if you need to reuse the fish for another group. Make sure to cover them with a damp towel to keep them in good shape. Have students share their artwork with their table partners or with the whole group, and have them point out the three body parts from earlier.

Optional Dissection

Don't be intimidated by dissection! Kids are way tougher than the world thinks they are. Once they have permission, they'll handle most of the dissection themselves. If you are looking for a gentler way to introduce dissection, try crawdads first and then move to fish.

Explain in advance what steps the group will take during the dissection, and explain what the conclusion will look like. For example: "At the end of the dissection, I'll give a one-minute warning, and then when I need your attention, I'll hold my hand up. Everyone will empty their hands, turn off their voices, and look at me."

If the dissection gets too loud, or it feels too much like *Lord of the Flies*, you can slow it down or end it easily if kids know what signals to watch and listen for. Dissections are gross, loud, and intense experiences. They rarely go exactly according to plan, so grant yourself a little flexibility.

Model the following steps for the students before letting them begin. It might help to draw a quick sketch on the board for them to refer to. Use scissors. Everybody wants to use a knife, but scissors are easier, safer, and more effective. Kids have more experience with scissors than scalpels (hopefully).

Start with a single scissor cut that removes the gill cover. This will expose the gill underneath. The gill is where oxygen exchange happens because fish don't have lungs.

Next, demonstrate how to carefully cut the fish open starting at the vent (anus) and cutting along the belly all the way to the chin. They shouldn't cut too deep because they'll damage the guts before they get to see them. If the shape of the fish makes it difficult to look inside, show them how to make a larger opening by making a vertical cut (from belly to backbone) in front of the abdominal cavity and also behind the abdominal cavity. Then they can lift away the abdominal wall that is blocking their view.

Have students look for:

* *Intestines.* They look like a wiggly noodle. Color varies with freshness.
* *Liver.* This is the dark red organ that is easy to find. It helps clean the blood.
* *Gills.* These are behind the gill slits covers. Gills are feathery looking and are usually red.

INTERESTING FACTS

The layer of slime that covers a fish protects it from infection and helps it slip through the water easily like wax on a surfboard.

Some fish have hard spines in their fins for protection. Their slime layer will make it really sting if they jab you! Some fish have venom in their spines that is strong enough to kill a person.

There are plenty of venomous snakes in the world, but there are more venomous fish than there are venomous snakes!

The scales of a fish have rings that can be counted to determine their age, kind of like a tree's rings.

Fish are dark on top and light on bottom to help with camouflage. If a predator is below them, the white belly blends in better with sunlight. If the predator is above them looking down, their dark back blends in with the shadows.

Gyotaku Tips

Less paint is definitely better, but students have trouble getting a feel for that until they've tried a few.

The cleaner you can keep your tray, the better the print. If you have paint smeared around the fish, the smear will print onto your paper, too.

Tissue paper works wonderfully if you have it because it is so easy to press down around the fish. In middle school, I've had careful students produce great work on Kleenex!

Fish aren't the only things you can print. I've had good luck with octopus too! See https://youtu.be/pi-N6UMRs8Y.

If you have time, show students how to produce multicolor prints. If you put several colors on the fish, your print won't be so monochromatic.

Finding Fish for Science Club

A fish market is a good place to get your specimens. *Make sure the scales are still on!* Fish skin still *looks* scaly after the scales are removed, so you'll need to touch the fish to be sure the scales are still there. Fish with skin instead of scales (like catfish) will not print as well.

If you want to go fishing and catch your own, go for it. Perch, brim, bass, crappie, carp, and any other fish with scales will work great as long as it'll fit onto your paper. After you catch your fish and get them home, put them in a freezer bag, and freeze your catch until you need them. They'll need to be thawed for the lab.

If you are close to a live-bait shop, check to see if they carry large minnows (two to three inches long). They can be frozen in advance of the meeting, and they work pretty well for large groups.

Pet stores often carry live goldfish that are sold as "feeder fish" for other pets. The larger ones (more than an inch or so) work fine, and if the students share specimens, it shouldn't break your budget.

A first grader prepares his newspaper tower for the oncoming hurricane

Civil Engineering with Newspaper Towers

● ● ●

NEED HELP WITH THIS LAB? *Ask me!* Find me on Twitter: @ TheFort_FW. Remember to tag your photos with #TSCHB so we can see what's going on in your lab!

Students will use limited resources to design, construct, and test a freestanding tower made out of newspaper and masking tape. Towers will be built for height and stability and will be tested with a wind load.

BACKGROUND

The charter of the Institute of Civil Engineers (founded in 1818) defines civil engineering as "the art of directing the great sources of power in nature for the use and convenience of man."[3]

Civil engineering is the area of construction that focuses on the design and building of structures that do not move from place to place. Roads, dams, buildings, canals, and bridges are all products of civil engineering. Civil engineering includes designing and building structures like houses or skyscrapers but can also include environmental projects like rerouting a river, designing a forest

---

3 (www.ice.org.uk)

or wetland, planning cities, or preparing for natural disasters like hurricanes, tornadoes, and earthquakes.

Civil engineering is an old practice, and it has its roots in the time when people stopped being nomads who constantly moved from place to place. As soon as they began to settle in one place, they needed homes for shelter, structures to store their food and protect their animals, and roads to travel to the next settlement.

There are lots of impressive examples of civil engineering from the past. They include:

* The Pyramids of Egypt
* The Roman Aqueducts
* The Great Wall of China
* The Catacombs in Rome
* The Parthenon in Athens, Greece

Modern examples of civil engineering projects would be:

* The Golden Gate Bridge
* The Sears Tower in Chicago
* The Eiffel Tower
* The Grand Canyon Skywalk
* The Sydney Opera House
* The Panama Canal

In the future, civil engineers will help us to use and reuse Earth's resources more efficiently, but those skills won't be limited to planet Earth! Civil engineers will be needed to design and build structures on the moon or other planets, and some civil engineers will likely become experts in terraforming. *Terra* means "earth." Terraforming is the process of changing the environment on other planets to be similar to planet Earth so humans can colonize the new planets. Right now, Mars seems to be the most likely candidate for terraforming, but the costs are too high, and the results are too uncertain to begin the process today.

In today's lab, we will be using a *five-step engineering process.* The steps are:

1. Designing and planning.
2. Building.
3. Testing what works and doesn't work.
4. Improving your idea.
5. Repeat.

It's easy to think of these five as a checklist that's finished at step 5, but it's better to imagine an arrow from step 5 leading right back to the top of the list. The ideas and improvements created during the engineering process can always be improved upon. Students who say "I'm finished!" have jumped out of the process. They need to jump back into the process and focus on how their design can be improved. This should be an encouragement to engineers who see that their first results don't work very well. Since the process is ongoing, their design will continue to improve! This process also helps students focus on improving their own design instead of competing over winning or losing with other groups. Competition is great, but it might be distracting.

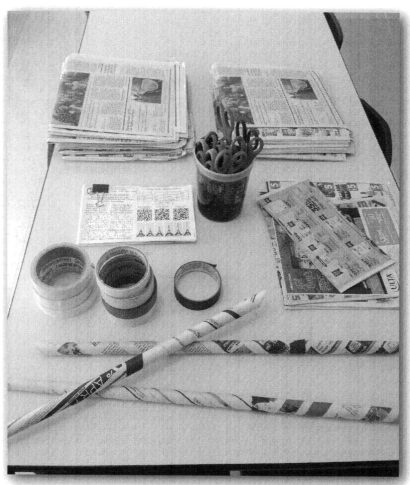

Newspaper tower lab supplies ready for Science Club!

Materials

Three Sunday editions of newspaper should do it for a normal-sized class. Your life will be easier if you separate the full sheets from the coupons and partial pages before beginning. If you are pressed for time, have the first qualified student who arrives separate them for you. If you have time and a budget, replace newspaper with packing paper from a moving company. Many companies that rent moving trucks also sell boxes and paper for wrapping up fragile things. This paper is larger and more uniform than newspaper. Crayons are useful because sometimes little fingers struggle with the dexterity to roll columns.

* Newspaper: six full sheets per pair or trio
* Masking tape
* Scissors
* Rulers or measuring tapes
* Optional: crayons or old markers to roll the papers around

Suggested Timing for One-Hour Lab

This is a framework; adjust as needed.

* Ten minutes: arrival and show-and-tell
* Ten minutes: introduction meeting on civil engineering information, construction terms, and supply and tool orientation
* Fifteen minutes: building and testing time (can be extended if students are deeply engaged)
* Five minutes: meeting on lessons learned, "I noticed/I wonder" comments, and helpful suggestions

* Fifteen minutes: second build time
* Five minutes: cleanup (scraps in the trash, tape off floor, and supplies collected and stacked)

Behavior Expectations

* Students can sword fight in Fencing Club. In Science Club, paper columns are for building, not fighting.
* Every member of the group is expected to help with construction and to help their group toward success.

Concepts/Useful Terms

Buckling is when a structure fails by bending or breaking.

Civil engineering is the term for building nonmoving structures like buildings, dams, and roads.

Column is a cylinder shape used as a support structure.

Deflection is the amount of movement a structure has from at rest position when moved by an outside force.

Lateral force is a force or push from the side. To help your students remember the root *lat*, remind them that your "lats" are muscles on the sides of your body, and in football, throwing the football sideways is called a *LATeral*.

Load is the weight that a structure must support. Loads are divided into two groups. Dead load is the weight that is supported all the time, like the weight of the tower itself. It doesn't change much. Live loads are moving, and they change, like lateral forces. Examples of live loads are workers walking in and out of a building or cars driving across a bridge.

Triangle is the strongest two-dimensional shape for building structures. The low number of edges, sides, and corners minimizes the areas of weakness.

PROCEDURE

After opening procedures are finished, gather students for a meeting, and explain the concept of civil engineering using the background information above.

Explain that we will be using a limited amount of supplies to build a structure for height and strength. We will be building structures as civil engineers in a hurricane-prone area. Explain the engineering process (in the background information).

Explain the parameters of the challenge:

Groups will receive three full sheets of newsprint and an arm's length of tape. (If you'd like them to practice measurement, say three feet of tape.) They will have fifteen minutes to construct their towers. Towers should be freestanding, not attached to the table or other surface.

Students will work in groups of two or three to design and build their newspaper towers, and they should make a plan within their group before building so that everybody is working together.

After fifteen minutes, engineers will measure the height of their tower and then test their tower with *lateral forces*. The lateral forces will be the students or teacher blowing their best hurricane winds at the tower from an arm's length away from the tower.

Note. Even if everyone conducts their own testing, the results should be pretty even. Kids with little lungs also have little arms, putting them closer to their target. Big kids with big lungs also have bigger arms, putting them farther away.

After testing, students will come back to the floor to discuss what worked, what didn't work, and what they discovered.

Model/Demonstrate These Two Skills for Students before Building
Tearing the Newsprint

The fibers of the paper are usually aligned in one direction. If they are vertical, the sheet will tear easily and cleanly with vertical tears but will be messy and chaotic when torn horizontally. (The only way to know if they are horizontal or vertical is to test a piece.) Show your engineers which way they can tear their paper to make smaller pieces quickly.

Rolling a Column

Lay the sheet on the floor, start at a corner, and roll diagonally toward the opposite corner. It may be helpful to start the column with a crayon. Lay the crayon on the corner, and roll it up in the column. You probably won't get the crayon back out, but the improvement to the columns is usually worth the loss. After the column is rolled, a single small piece of tape can hold it together. If students need to have multiple columns of the exact same length, they should make their columns and then trim their tips with scissors to make them uniform.

After taking questions, dismiss to tables to begin building.

Build for fifteen minutes. This is the testing stage where students will be gathering data about what works and what doesn't work. During this time, circulate through the work area, solving supply issues and offering support. Keep track of the time and provide a ten-minute warning, a five-minute warning, and a two-minute warning.

At the end of fifteen minutes, have students stop building, measure their towers, and then test them by blowing hard on them from arm's length. Then have students return to the floor to discuss their results.

Have students raise their hand if their tower was at least ten inches tall. Raise it if your tower was at least eleven inches tall; then twelve, thirteen, fourteen, and so on. Keep counting higher until all hands stay down. Ask the group with the highest measurement to describe their strategies for the group. Use this time to introduce and/or reinforce the concepts and key terms for civil engineering.

Ask the students to share what they discovered or noticed as they built and if possible to use the key terms to help them in their discussions. If there are many hands raised, instead of having the students share one at a time, have the students turn to their neighbors and explain.

Ask students what part they found challenging or difficult while building. One other useful question is, "If you were going to help a kindergartner build one of these towers, what advice would you give them to help them be successful?"

Explain to the students that they will be using what they learned from building and from the discussion to build a second, better tower. It is up to the teacher whether they are adding to their first tower or beginning a brand-new one.

Release the group back to their work areas, and give them fifteen minutes for second build. Give the same time warnings as the first build. At the end, have students measure and test their designs to see if they improved. If students want to keep the towers, they can *if the entire group agrees on who gets to keep it.* If it isn't unanimous, nobody gets dibs.

At the end, have groups clean up their work space and toss scraps into the trash.

Tips

Remind students that this is not a spelling test! *Copying your neighbor's work is encouraged!* If they see something they like, they should copy it, and if someone copies their work, they should be proud.

If students are young, unmotivated, or lack confidence, get them moving with the following strategies:

* Roll a column, and gift it to someone who is having trouble.
* Make design suggestions to get them started.
* Alter your plan to have one longer build session instead of two shorter builds.
* Provide extra materials to keep them moving.

Extension Activities

Have students construct three-dimensional geometric shapes from newspaper columns. A triangular pyramid is the fastest. Cubes and triangular prisms are also interesting.

Instead of building a structure for height, have them design and build a structure that reaches out over the edge of a table. Challenge students to see how far they can extend a structure off the edge of a table.

Trusses, struts, and braces can be taught and added. These structures can be attached to the table.

Have towers support a load. Tennis balls work great. Have students build towers like normal, but modify the challenge so that it must hold the load as high in the air as possible. It's pretty challenging, so don't start your second graders with this one!

At the middle and high school level, students can be challenged to design a structure, stool, or chair that will hold a student at least six inches off the floor. This takes longer than a single period, but the results can be impressive.

Studying Cephalopods through Squid Dissection

● ● ●

Need help with this lab? *Ask me!* Find me on Twitter: @ TheFort_FW. Remember to tag your photos with #TSCHB so we can see what's going on in your lab!

Background

Squids are a type of cuttlefish. These mollusks are related to the octopus, nautilus, and the extinct ammonite. These jet-powered predators are fierce hunters with sharp beaks, multiple brains, razor-sharp suction cups, built-in smoke bombs, and the best camouflage in nature. Their camo is *waaaay* better than the best chameleon.

To understand their camouflage skills, imagine being able to wear a video screen for your skin. You could stand in front of any background and switch the color pattern of your camouflage to blend in with anything! Similar to pixels on a video screen, a squid's skin is covered in little dots of color called CHROMOATO-PHORES. *Chromato* refers to "color," and *-phore* means "carrier." These dots come in the primary colors of red, yellow, and blue, along with white, brown/black, and iridescent. When it's time for the squid to appear blue, muscles in their skin will open the blue dots and close the other colors. If they need to be green, they can mix blue and yellow dots! The coolest part of this color change is it happens instantly, and the colors can move around the skin! Imagine if you could make your freckles surf all over your skin! And don't forget those iridescent dots. With those, you could make your freckles reflect like a mirror and then go dull like the sidewalk. If you switched back and forth quickly, you'd look just like rippling water.

The fabulous color changes are only half of the camouflage skills of some cephalopods, though. An octopus can also change the *texture* of its skin to match the rocks, coral, seaweed, or sand nearby. They have special muscles in their skin that let them change how smooth or rough it is. It would be as if you went into the woods, hugged a tree, switched your skin color to match the browns, grays, and greens of the trunk, *and then* you tensed your muscles so that your skin popped out in rough, ridgy bumps and cracks just like the bark or the tree you are hugging. *In-vis-i-ble!*

As squids hunt, they reach out their tentacles, and when they find prey, they latch on with their suction cups. This action is *lightning fast.* Cephalopods have what are called distributed brains. This means that besides one-third of their brain neurons collected together in their head, they also have lobes of neurons behind their eyes, and two-thirds of their brain neurons are spread throughout their tentacles. This makes them superfast hunters, because when their tentacle encounters food, the message doesn't have to travel to their head for processing before they grab. Their tentacle does its own thinking and just grabs. (Maybe squid kids can get their tentacles to do their homework for them while their head brain-plays video games.) Some squids have suckers that have sharp edges around the rim, so that when they attach their suction cups to their prey, the suckers slice into its skin. Sperm whales are often covered in battle scars from the sharp tentacles of the giant squids that they like to eat.

When the squid has captured prey with its tentacle, it pulls it to its mouth. The mouth is a sharp beak like a parrot has, and it can slice off bites of food. The beak, usually a black or dark brown color, is in the middle of all the legs, so you'll have to move the legs around to find it.

Materials

Whole squid specimens come frozen from the fish market and are inexpensive. A box to supply a whole class costs as much as a fast-food lunch. They are also available at some Asian markets. Make sure that they are whole/complete and not just the tentacles. They will need to be thawed before the lab. It's fine to substitute octopus for this lab, but they are harder to find still intact. If you are going to use squid or octopus for display, they are usually on ice, and kids love examining them.

* Whole squid specimens: one per pair or trio of students
* Dissection tray or plate
* Hand lenses
* Hand soap
* Plastic butter knives *or* student scissors
* Baby wipes
* Spoons
  Optional
* A pair of pliers for the teacher to use during dissection (needle-nose pliers work great)
* A large squid or octopus specimen to use for display

Suggested Timing for One-Hour Lab
(This is a framework; adjust as needed.)

* Five minutes: arrival and show-and-tell
* Twenty minutes: introduction and background meeting—tools, external structures, using our senses, and expectations
* Fifteen minutes: exploration/observation in small groups (if interest is shown for longer, *extend this time*)
* Ten minutes (on the floor): discussing how to open/dissect, what to look for, and student questions
* Five minutes: dissection (look for pen, intestines, ink, stomach, and siphon)
* Five minutes: cleanup (*all* scraps in the trash, trays and tools cleaned and dried, and tables wiped)

Behavior Expectations

* Students will help others feel comfortable. Use specimens for science, not for scaring people.
* Specimens are for learning science. We will learn from them, not treat them like toys.
* Use the right tool for the job: hand lenses for looking and spoons and fingers for touching.
* Keep your area neat. Don't make a mess just for entertainment.

Concepts
A squid's camouflage helps it hide, hunt, and communicate.

Dissecting means "to take something apart to learn about its pieces."

Procedure

Have students gather together (probably on the floor) for background information on the squid. Explain that you will be dissecting CEPHALOPODS today. *Cephalo* means "head," and *pod* means "foot" or "leg." Ask the students to think of animals that look like a head stuck on top of a set of legs. After a few guesses, give them a clue: hold one hand in a fist to be a head, and use the fingers of your other hand to be wiggly legs attached underneath. You can make a fairly convincing octopus that way.

Provide squid background information as your timing allows (see above). This will be the best attentive listening you will get from them during this lab, so make the most of it.

Explain that in the first part of the lab, students will be exploring the external body parts of the squid. They should locate the following:

* CHROMATOPHORES. The little dots of color on a CEPHALO-POD's skin
* TENTACLES. The arms on a cephalopod
* BEAK. The sharp, moving mouth parts of a CEPHALOPOD

Explain the tools they'll be using (hand lens and plastic spoons), and model how you would and *would not* like them to be used. For example, hand lenses are held near the specimen, not near your eye.

Send students to their tables, and pass out the supplies. Circulate around the room guiding and monitoring the lab. Let this exploration extend as long as their interest holds.

After students have completed their initial investigation, call them back to the floor to meet again (leaving tools and squids at the table). If time allows, discuss what they noticed, and what they are wondering about the squids. Explain that they will be dissecting next and that inside of the squid they should look for several specific structures:

* PEN (in a squid/cuttlefish, not in an octopus). It's the long, flat cartilage that supports the squid's shape. It resembles an old-fashioned feather pen.
* INTESTINES. The organ that digests the squid's food. They are part of the digestive tract and are sort of the midway point in the food consumption process. (The mouth is the beginning, and the anus is the end.)
* SIPHON. The muscular tube that acts as a jet to move the squid from place to place. Water enters around the mantle and then is forced through the siphon like a squirt gun, shooting the squid through the water. The siphon is also called a HYPONOME.

EXPLAIN THESE STEPS *BEFORE* BEGINNING THE DISSECTION

Students will remove and examine the pen first. The pen can be pulled out by locating the tip of the pen on top of the mantle/hood (it feels like a hard bump above their head), and scraping off a piece of the soft tissue to get to the cartilage underneath. Younger kids might have trouble getting started, so show them how to feel on the squid's mantle for the hard tip of the pen and then pinch off a bit of the soft tissue, using your thumbnail. With the tip of the pen exposed, grab the tip of the pen by pinching with your thumbnail again and boldly pulling it out like a long splinter. The pen is usually clear, and it's fine for kids to keep them because they will dry before they stink. If the pen is difficult to remove with your fingernails, use pliers. (If you have enough squids, practice with one or two before class starts.)

After students have removed and examined the pen, they will open the mantle with the plastic knife. Squids are soft, so plastic knives work great. Student scissors work great, too. Students will insert the knife under the mantle and open the "belly" of the squid.

They can tell if a squid specimen is male or female during the dissection by looking inside toward the tail. The gonad is white in males and clear in females.

After explaining the dissection procedure, send students back to begin their dissection. Rotate around the lab, monitoring progress, and lending a hand where needed. At the end, have students clean their tools and toss specimens into the trash.

Interesting Facts

It is fine to share octopus facts in a squid lab and vice versa.

If you ever go to a restaurant and order calamari, you will be eating today's lab. Calamari rings are the squid's mantle sliced and cooked (often fried).

Squids do have blood, but it doesn't look like human blood. Humans have iron in their blood, which makes it red. Squid blood doesn't use iron. It uses copper, so their blood is blue-green in color. When they die, their blood quickly turns gray without oxygen.

An octopus normally has eight legs (*octo* means "eight"), but there have been cases where an octopus was born with six legs, in effect creating a HEXAPUS. (It's probably a birth defect rather than a new species.)

Octopuses are supersmart compared to other mollusks. They can open jars, hunt on dry land, and bend the shape and movement of their bodies to match the form of sharks, crabs, and rocks. (Do yourself a favor and go look up the mimic octopus on YouTube.)

Cuttlefish bone, or cuttlebone, is often sold in pet stores. Birds, reptiles, and rodents like to nibble it for calcium. In the past, cuttlebone has been ground up into powder and used in toothpaste and other abrasive polishes. Cuttlebone can withstand very high heat, so jewelers sometimes use it to cast designs. They carve the shape they want in the cuttlebone and then pour in the blazing-hot liquid metal.

Squids make great monsters in literature. They have made appearances in *20,000 Leagues under the Sea* (Jules Verne, 1870), in *Moby Dick* (Henry Melville, 1851), and in *The Cay* (Theodore Taylor, 1969). In Disney's *Pirates of the Caribbean* series (films released in 2003, 2006, 2007, 2011), Davy Jones has an octopus for a face, and the Cracken is a giant squid. In Disney's *The Littlest Mermaid* (1989), Ursula the witch is an evil octopus. In *Finding Dory* (2016) Hank the octopus (he's really a septapus) showcases the awesome power of cephalopod camo!

Some people confuse the terms *cuttlefish* and *squid*. It can be doubly confusing, since cuttlefish aren't really even fish! Squids are one type of cuttlefish. Cuttlefish is the name of the large group, and squids, octopus, and nautilus are all types of cuttlefish.

In the lab, the octopus can solve problems like opening child-proof bottles or escaping from tanks to sneak around the lab while nobody is there. Sometimes they'll slip into other aquariums and eat the fish. They are even smart enough to get back into their own tanks before they get caught.

An octopus can bend, twist, and stretch its body better than Elastigirl in *The Incredibles* (2004). They can pour their own body through any hole that their beak can fit through. Use your hands to make a circle the size of *your* mouth. Imagine trying to crawl through a hole that size!

Octopuses are not very social. They tend to spend time alone, which works out pretty well because they are cannibals. Humans aren't the only ones that think cephalopods are delicious!

An octopus's ability to use objects as tools is a sign of high intelligence, but their intelligence is spread throughout their body. Even an hour after the main brain of an octopus has died, their tentacles are still "smart" enough to pull away from danger.

Octopus armor. As if all the other superpowers were not enough, octopuses have been observed in the ocean carrying around two halves of a coconut shell like a human would carry a purse. When they sensed danger, they climbed inside, clapped the two halves together around them, and held them in place with their suckers. They had the benefit of coconut camouflage, as well as thick armor plating!

A young botanist prepares to send his specimens into the future

Plant-Press Time Machines

● ● ●

NEED HELP WITH THIS LAB? *Ask me*! Find me on Twitter: @ TheFort_FW. Remember to tag your photos with #TSCHB so we can see what's going on in your lab!

BACKGROUND

Every human on Earth depends on plants for survival. Most of what we eat is either part of a plant or it's from an animal that ate plants. Nurturing and studying plant life is essential for our survival!

Imagine what the area around your school looked like one hundred, two hundred, or even three hundred years ago. Imagine what animals, people, and plants lived and grew right where you are sitting. What if there was a person standing right on this spot two hundred years ago, and he or she was able to gather samples of the leaves and flowers from this very spot, put them into a time machine, and send them forward in time to your hands so that you could open it and see what the plants were like, on this very spot before your grandparents were born? Well, that sort of time machine is not imaginary. That sort of time travel is possible. Today we are going to build that time machine, so that you can send messages into the future. This time machine is called a plant press, and it allows us to capture the specimens of today and send them into the future.

Botany is the study of plants, and as students work as botanists in this lab, they'll learn that there are many types of plants, and they often have interesting abilities.

They might have:

- *Defenses* like spikes, sharp edges, poisonous juices, bitter tastes, itchy hairs, disabling oils, or shooting darts
- *Hunting tools* like snapping jaws, sticky or slippery traps, enticing fruit and flowers, and delicious-smelling bait
- *Reproduction tricks* like parachutes, catapults, hitchhiking, sailing the high seas, fishhooks, lassos, Velcro, and flying spears
- *Survival tricks* like becoming a parasite, hiding in animal poop, communicating with other plants, going for a walk, making friends with an animal, or entering suspended animation

MATERIALS

Don't be scared of the hardware store! If you don't understand which hardware you need, just ask an employee. Think of the store as a library and the staff as librarians of building and fixing. They'll help you figure it out!

Get wooden slats from the local big-box home-improvement store. Find the cheapest version of eight-inch-wide fence pickets they have, and ask the staff to cut them into ten-inch-long sections for you. Sometimes they charge for the cut, but they'll usually do it for free for educators. The fewer the knotholes, cracks, and warped boards, the better. You get to choose the boards, and you are allowed to be selective. (One six-foot-long board will yield seven, ten-inch slats.)

One-and-three-quarters-inch length bolts work well, but any size will work as long as they are long enough to reach through two boards plus a pinch of papers and plants in the middle. Bolts that are size (diameter) #8-32 work fine but there is nothing magical about that size.

Any size of washers will work as long as the bolt fits through the hole and the nut doesn't.

Sometimes metal nuts come in a set with the bolts, and you just buy them together. Other times, you choose them separately. Hex nuts are great. Wing nuts are even better.

Make sure that the drill battery is charged, or use one that plugs in. Nothing takes the wind out of your sails more than getting shut down with a dead battery mid lab.

You can have students gather their own leaf and flower specimens, take them on a nature walk, or provide specimens for them. If you provide the specimens, the wire cutters are your best friend for taking small sample branches from trees, bushes, and shrubbery. Also, florists with flowers just past their prime are a great resource for flowers to press. Just ask them in advance for any flowers that have gone wilty. They will either be free or cheap. Flowers will press really well if they lay flat. Fat, lumpy buds are hard to press.

- Wire cutters
- Envelopes
- Crayons
- Hand lenses
- Scissors
- Manila paper (about four sheets per student)
- Ten-inch wooden slats (two per student)

- Bolts to hold the plant press together (two per student)
- Washers (four per student)
- Metal nuts to tighten onto the bolts (two per student)
- A drill to make a hole large enough for the bolts to go through
- Leaf and flower specimens

Suggested Timing for One-Hour Lab
(This is a framework; adjust as needed.)

- Five minutes: arrival and show-and-tell
- Fifteen minutes: introduction and background meeting—tools, time travel, producers and consumers, photosynthesis, chlorophyll, and student expectations
- Fifteen minutes: building and decorating plant presses
- Ten minutes (on the floor): meeting to discuss how to put plants in the paper folders, what to look for, and student questions
- Ten minutes: adding plants to their presses
- Five minutes: cleanup (*all* scraps in the trash, trays and tools cleaned and dried, and tables wiped)

Behavior Expectations

- Use the right tool for the right job: hand lenses for looking, drills for drilling, and so forth.
- Keep your area neat. There will be some mess, so make sure to clean up your area as needed. Don't make a mess just for entertainment.

* Share specimens with other students.
* If you are collecting leaves as a group, collect thoughtfully. Collect in a way that won't destroy plants or gardens. If you are unsure, ask your instructor before collecting.

CONCEPTS

* Leaf presses are useful for sending leaves into the future for further study. They work by protecting specimens from decomposition, moisture, and pests.
* Leaves produce food for their plant using sunlight. The process is called PHOTOSYNTHESIS. *Photo* means "light," and *synthesis* means "build."
* The food they create is called chlorophyll. It's the green smears on your pants when you get a grass stain.

PROCEDURE

To build the plant presses, students will take their two boards and stack them onto one another. They will drill a hole at one end to hold a bolt and then drill a second hole at the other end to hold the second bolt. The two bolt holes need to be far enough apart that your manila paper fits between them (at least eight and a half inches, if you are using 8½″ x 11″ paper).

Let the students do most of the drilling if possible. If long hair is pulled back, drills aren't particularly dangerous, and students who use them enjoy a strong sense of empowerment regardless of how old they are. Just hold the drill straight up, and don't drill the desks, counters, or floor.

After the drilling, have students use the washers, bolts, and nuts to fasten the two boards together. (If you are looking at a properly assembled press, you will see two boards with washers up against the wood on top and bottom, with a bolt pushed through, and a nut holding it together. Or from bottom to top, you would see bolt, washer, board, board, washer, and nut.)

Next, they will make their paper folders by taking their stack of manila papers and folding them in half to make 8½″ x 5½″ folders. Some people call that fold hamburger style. The folded pages will all nest together, and they will get inserted in between the boards of the plant press after the leaves and flowers are laid in. At this point, the presses are complete. Some students will finish before others, so it will be helpful to have markers or colored pencils out for them to decorate their plant press while they wait. When everyone has completed their build, move to the floor for a quick meeting on how to use the presses.

Show students how to select a leaf or a flower and lay it flat in one of the folders. It's fine to add multiple specimens to one folder, but try not to overlap them. Plants and leaves that will lay flat are great, but lumpy things like sticks, hard buds, and seeds will not press well.

Students don't need to totally separate their bolts and boards to add specimens. (It's a good way to lose pieces.) Instead, show students how to just loosen the nuts on their presses so that they can slip their specimen folders in and out. Also, students tend to pull out one folder at a time, but you can show them that it is much easier to pull out the whole nested folder stack, add a specimen, and then put the whole stack back into the press.

Remind them to write a date and location next to their specimens— time travel isn't very fun if you don't know how far you've gone!

After adding specimens to their press, they'll tighten the nuts to press the specimens firmly inside. The paper will absorb moisture from the specimens, and the tight storage will protect from pests that like to nibble leaves. When students have finished adding specimens, they can continue to decorate their press. Make sure their press has their name on it and the date they built it.

Pro tip: Remind students not to lay their presses on their parents' pretty furniture. Those bolts and nuts will scratch wood surfaces pretty quickly.

Alternative Plant Presses

It's possible to build presses out of cardboard and rubber bands with newspaper folders in between. These are faster and cheaper, but they don't last as long, and they aren't as impressive. If you need a load of plant presses quickly and you don't have much of a budget, two Sunday papers, some rubber bands, and a quick trip to the recycling Dumpster for cardboard will get you up and running.

Extension Activity: Leaf Rubbings

Another great way to study the shapes and patterns of leaves is to create rubbings on paper. Usually you take a leaf, lay it on the table, lay paper over it, and use your pencil or a crayon to gently color back and forth over the whole leaf. (You can do the same thing with a penny.) The problem with this sort of arrangement is that it's hard for students to hold their paper still while coloring. Moving the paper creates a blurred double image of the leaf.

An easy solution for this is to use paper envelopes instead of flat paper.

Have students place their leaf inside an envelope and then close the flap. (Don't seal it up.) Then lay the envelope flat, and do your rubbings on the envelope. When they accidentally move their artwork, it won't matter. The leaf will move, too, and everything will stay in alignment. If you don't have envelopes, have the students fold a piece of typing paper in half, and lay their leaf into the fold for a similar effect.

Rubbings can be used to create artwork, can be added to journals, or can be glued onto the plant presses as decorations.

INTERESTING FACTS

Leaves breathe for the plant. They lose quite a bit of water in the process. You can observe the water loss by putting a clear plastic bag over leaves on the end of a tree branch and then use a wire tie to close up the bag around the branch. As the leaves give off water, it will begin to accumulate on the inside of the bag.

The *boquila* vine, also known as the "chameleon vine," has the odd ability to grow on other trees or bushes and then mimic the shapes, colors, and even the size of the leaves on that tree! If one long Boquila vine grows across several different types of tree, each section of the Boquila vine can mimic the leaves of the plant that are touching that section of vine.

If you hold up a wooden stool and ask most people (teachers included) what it's made of, they'll say wood. But if you press them to go deeper (what is the *wood* made of?), they'll be stumped. *Wood is nearly all carbon.* (The leaves and stems are, too.) Many folks know that humans breathe in oxygen and breathe out carbon dioxide, also known as CO_2 (one carbon atom attached to two oxygen atoms). They also know that plants take in the carbon dioxide and release oxygen, also known as O_2 (two oxygen atoms linked together). What most folks miss is that the only difference between CO_2 and O_2 is the single carbon atom that our bodies add to the O_2 and the plants strip away. *As plants grow larger and larger, they are using those captured carbon atoms as their building blocks.* If a dead plant is decomposed or burned, it releases that carbon back into the air as CO_2. Some scientists suggest using plants to reduce CO_2 in the atmosphere. Simply plant large corn crops, let them grow, capture lots of carbon, and then bury the plants underground! After a couple of years, millions of tons of CO_2 would be moved from the atmosphere into the dirt.

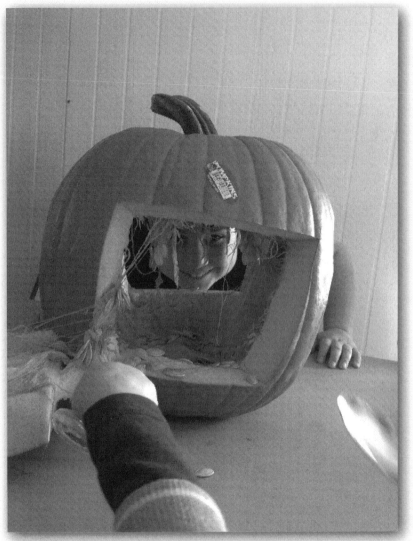

A young scientist dissecting her pumpkin with a friend

Squash Fear of Biology with a Pumpkin Dissection

● ● ●

Need help with this lab? *Ask me!* Find me on Twitter: @ TheFort_FW. Remember to tag your photos with #TSCHB so we can see what's going on in your lab!

Caution: Some students have skin sensitivity to pumpkin goo. If a student complains of itching hands, have the student wash his or her hands and use the spoons for handling the goo.

Background

Pumpkins, gourds, squashes, and other members of *Cucurbita* are a great way to enjoy plant dissections. They can grow in nearly every color imaginable (orange, yellow, blue, green, white, red, etc.), and the color patterns can be solid, striped, polka dots, or even lacy webs of colors. They generally have firm flesh, large seeds, and interesting shapes and colors.

Squashes and humans have an intertwined history that goes back several thousand years because growing them is a great way to cultivate food quickly and efficiently. The seeds are high in oil and protein. They store well when they are kept cool and dry, so they were also a useful food source for early North American settlers. Gourds can be used as vessels, utensils, and even birdhouses!

Some gourds do grow in the wild, but they tend to be very bitter. In the past, these bitter gourds may have been a food source for large mammals that have since gone extinct.

Pumpkins vines can be nearly fifty feet long, and students will be interested to know that pumpkins are a type of berry. Sizes vary widely, ranging from as small as two inches across to the world-record-sized pumpkins that are over 2,000 pounds (930 kilograms) each!

Pumpkin vines produce both male and female flowers, with the males producing pollen, and the female flowers turning into the fruit once the pollen fertilizes it. Fertilization usually occurs when bees fly from flower to flower with pollen on their legs, but it can also be done by hand with a paintbrush or cotton swab.

In this lab, the terms *pumpkin*, *gourd*, and *squash* will all be used interchangeably.

MATERIALS

Small pie pumpkins work great for pairs; larger pumpkins can accommodate three kids. Pairing students together focuses them better and requires fewer specimens to manage. Size, color, and texture are teacher's discretion. If you time this lab between Halloween and Thanksgiving, *pumpkins will be free or really cheap.* Contact a produce manager or farmer's market around October 31, and ask them what they'll be doing with the pumpkins that don't sell. Metal spoons are best, and strong plastic ones will work.

* Pumpkins and gourds: one per pair or trio of kids
* Trash bags
* Table wipes

- Metal butter knives
- Hand lenses
- Paper towels
- Trays or platters to contain specimens
- Hammers or wooden blocks to drive knives into the pumpkin
- Spoons

OPTIONAL TOOLS

- Rulers make great scrapers for cleaning up desks and tables.
- Spray bottles help to loosen dried goo.
- Newspaper place mats really help minimize mess.

SUGGESTED TIMING FOR ONE-HOUR LAB

This is a framework; adjust as needed. Do cleanup early, because *it can easily take longer than expected* with this lab.

- Ten minutes: arrival and show-and-tell
- Ten minutes: introduction meeting—background information, pumpkin anatomy, counting seeds, tools, using our senses, and expectations
- Twenty minutes: dissection in small groups (if interest is shown for longer, extend this time)
- Ten minutes: cleanup (*all* pumpkin trash put away, seeds and goo swept up, trays and tools cleaned and dried, and tables wiped)
- Ten minutes: wrap-up discussion—"I noticed/I wonder" statements, fun facts, extension activities for home, and dismissal

Behavior Expectations

- Knives *will not* be used for stabbing or striking. The tip of the knife will be pressed to the pumpkin and *then* driven in by striking the handle. Pumpkins are really tough, and a deflected stab will end up stuck in your neighbor's hand. (Reinforce this during the lab by quietly confiscating misused knives and then returning them to the overeager scientists after a sixty-second cooling-off period.)
- Stay at your work area so you won't drip seeds and slime all around the room.
- Even though it's fun to fling, pumpkin goo will not be thrown or flicked at people.

Concepts

- Squashes have similar characteristics to their parents and to each other.
- Squashes are PRODUCERS that are a good food source for people and other animals.
- Squashes reproduce from seeds grown within the fruit.

Procedure

Setup. You may need to partially precut pumpkins before the meeting begins for younger students. Fourth graders can usually open pumpkins independently. Leave the specimens assembled for the students to open. If prep time is short, you can assist younger students during the lab.

After opening procedures, begin by providing background information on pumpkins, possibly at the floor. Explain the parts of the pumpkin and the tools students will use for dissecting their specimens. Model for them the right way to open their pumpkin with the butter knife. *No stabbing!* They'll place the tip of the knife against the pumpkin and then tap it into the pumpkin with a hammer or a block of wood. If hammers or wood are unavailable, show students how to wrap one hand around the handle so the tip of the handle is hidden and then use their other hand to palm strike down against their knife hand to drive the knife in (striking the handle directly with your hand is uncomfortable). After the knife is in the pumpkin, they should press the handle back and forth like a lever to pull the blade through the pumpkin. (Sawing is not effective with butter knives.) After they have cut a complete opening in their pumpkin, they'll pry the top off and begin removing seeds and goo.

Show students how to use trays and newspaper to contain the mess, and model the correct way to use hand lenses (close to the specimen, not up against your eye).

Explain the cleanup procedure *before* you begin the dissection. Assign cleanup roles now. For example: "At cleanup time, Mark will gather the hand lenses, Heather and Connor will collect and wash knives, Hayden will bring the rolling trash can to your table, and Kara Jo will collect and wash spoons. Everyone else will clean the tables and floors."

Have students predict how many seeds will be in their gourd *before opening* their gourds. Have them write that prediction on the side of their pumpkin. After opening their pumpkin, they can sort the goo and the seeds and count. They can use hands or spoons to dissect. If you want to help students overcome fear of messy hands, postpone passing out spoons until they ask for them.

Release students to their tables, and tell them who they will be working with. ("I would like you and you to work together on this pumpkin.") During dissection, the teacher should rotate around the room monitoring and assisting. If students are pressed for time, provide time warnings so they don't get surprised by having to stop mid-dissection.

Make sure to end with enough time to clean up. After cleanup, use any remaining time to hold a wrap-up discussion.

EXTENSION ACTIVITIES

* Prepare and eat seeds.
* Make pie.
* Fill a pumpkin with dirt to sprout seeds.
* Set up a pumpkin to observe decomposition for a week or so (definitely outside).
* Tag team with the art teacher to hold a pumpkin-carving activity.

INTERESTING FACTS

Pumpkins, watermelons, and cantaloupes are related closely enough that they can be crossed together to make a hybrid plant that shares characteristics of several plants! When you are planting a garden, put them far apart from each other so you don't accidentally get a cantamelon, a pumpermelon, or a waterlope.

Big pumpkins are big business! When a pumpkin sets a world record for being the biggest, the seeds from that pumpkin become very valuable. A single seed can be sold for thirty-five dollars. An average pumpkin has around three hundred seeds. (Bigger pumpkins can have even more.) Three hundred seeds at thirty-five dollars each would mean the pumpkin would be worth over $10,000!

The word *squash* comes from the Narragansett word *askutas-quash*, which means "green thing eaten raw."

Pumpkin seeds can be eaten raw, roasted, pressed into oil, or ground into flour. The flowers and young leaves can also be eaten as long as they are not bitter tasting.

Wild gourds are usually extremely bitter. In some parts of Mexico, the bitter juices are used as a topical ointment applied to the mother to help wean children off breast milk.

Pumpkin seeds have been used to get rid of tapeworms living in the gut.

If you want a carved pumpkin to last longer without rotting, give it a bath to kill the molds and fungi that break it down. Mix a teaspoon of bleach with a gallon of water, and dunk your pumpkin in the solution. You can also use a spray bottle to sterilize your pumpkin if it's too large to dunk.

A pile of live Blue Crabs at the fish market

The Blue-Crabby Labby

● ● ●

Caution: Crabs are shellfish. Students with shellfish allergies should not handle them. Crabs have sharp points and are not clean. Any pokes or cuts should be washed and bandaged.

BACKGROUND

Blue crabs are a type of crustacean that lives in salt water. They are DECAPODS. *Deca* means "ten," and *pod* means "leg." They are also ARTHROPODS. *Arthr-* means "joint," and *-pod* still means "leg." Their official name is *Callinectes sapidus*, which means "beautiful, savory swimmer."

Blue crab predators include humans, sharks, stingrays, eels, bass, trout, octopus, and other blue crabs.

Blue crabs have been eaten in the Americas for hundreds of years, but until technology for refrigeration was developed in the eighteen hundreds, only people close to the ocean had a chance to enjoy them. Everyone else missed out because crabs go bad too quickly to ship without refrigeration.

Crabs are covered in armor called an EXOSKELETON. It gives the crab's body support because crabs have no bones. It also protects them from danger because crabs are delicious, and lots of animals want to eat them. The exoskeleton of a crab has lots of different pretty colors in it, especially reds and blues. When a crab is cooked for dinner (usually by boiling), the blue colors break down and disappear. That's why crabs on your dinner plate are orange and red.

LIFE CYCLE

Females carry their eggs on their bellies (up to eight million). When they first hatch, crabs are called ZOEA (*zoe-EE-yuh*). They are about a millimeter long and are too wimpy to swim around. They just go where the current takes them while eating plankton. After they have molted a few times, they grow into MEGALOPA (pronounced as *mega-LOPE-a*). They are about three millimeters long, and they can swim, but they hang around the bottom of the water, looking for food. Megalopa look like tiny crayfish or lumpy lobsters. After several more molts, they grow to be *JUVENILE CRABS*. They finally look like crabs, and they hunt and eat the same diet as an adult. When they are about one year old, they grow into the ADULT stage, where they can reproduce/lay eggs. Blue crabs live about three to four years. The females only mate once and only when their shell is soft.

HABITAT

They can be found in the Atlantic Ocean nearly all the way up the East Coast. They are in the Gulf of Mexico and are often caught by Texas fishermen. They can be caught with a fishing line, a net, or a crab pot.

MATERIALS

One crab per two to three students increases engagement, and it costs less money than one per student. Get crabs live from the grocery store or fish market and put them in the freezer. Freezing is a humane way to prepare arthropods for study—they are cold blooded, so their systems ease to a stop in the freezer. There's not the drama of the boiling cook pot you just saved them from. To set up the lab, run them under warm water to thaw.

At the elementary or intermediate level, no scalpels or scissors are needed because crabs come apart without them. At the high school level, a more detailed investigation may warrant sharp tools.

* Blue crab specimens
* Trays or plates
* Spoons
* Hand lenses
* Hand soap
* Baby wipes
* Pliers

SUGGESTED TIMING FOR ONE-HOUR LAB
(This is a framework; adjust as needed.)

* Ten minutes: arrival and show-and-tell
* Ten minutes: introduction meeting—tools, external structures, using our senses, and expectations
* Fifteen minutes: exploration/observation in small groups (if interest is shown for longer, *extend this time*)
* Ten minutes (on the floor): lecture of blue crab life cycle, habitat, gender, and how to open/dissect

- Ten minutes: dissection (look for gills, intestines, heart, and stomach)
- Five minutes: cleanup (*all* scraps in the trash, trays and tools cleaned and dried, and tables wiped)

BEHAVIOR EXPECTATIONS

- Students will help others feel comfortable. Use specimens for science, not for scaring people.
- Specimens are for learning science. We will learn from them, not treat them like toys.
- Use the right tool for the job: hand lenses for looking and spoons and fingers for touching.
- Keep your area neat. Don't make a mess just for entertainment.

CONCEPTS

- Blue crabs have adaptations that help them thrive within their environment.
- When a person eats (consumes) a crab, the energy within the crab is transferred to the person.

PROCEDURE

Begin with a floor meeting to provide background information about the blue crab. Explain habitats, tools students will be using, and student expectations and then explain the first four body parts that you would like students to find:

Mandibles. These are the crab's mouth parts. They don't move up and down like a person's jaws. Instead, they move sideways like an ant. Humans have a single mandible. It's the bone in your chin.

Lateral spines. These are the two fearsome spines on the sides of the crab's carapace (shell). There is one on each side. They provide some protection from predators. The small, ridge-like spikes along the front of the shell are not lateral spines. They are called teeth, but they aren't used for chewing.

Abdomen. If you flip the crab onto its back, you can find the abdomen. It looks like a tail that is pressed tightly against the belly of the crab. You can tell a crab's gender by looking at its abdomen. A male crab's abdomen looks like the Washington Monument. An adult female's abdomen looks like the Capitol Dome. A juvenile female's is like a triangle. You should have all males because fishermen usually throw females back to support the crab life cycle.

Swimming legs. The pair of legs closest to the abdomen is adapted for swimming. They are like paddles for pushing and steering a crab through the water. They aren't very useful for walking, but the six walking legs take care of that task. Crabs that live on land don't have swimming legs.

Release students to their seats, and pass out specimens and tools. As students examine their specimen, move around the room asking guiding questions and answering student requests. *The experiences in this portion of the lab are the most valuable, so if their interest holds, let them go longer than you had planned.*

Pro tip: If you have a class that is reluctant to touch the specimens, ask them if they have ever felt a crab before *while you reach over and feel it.* When you finally see a student touch a crab, ask him or her what it felt like. Whatever the answer is, the student's friends will want to confirm by touching the crab as well. This modeling of how to touch the crab will be more effective than just telling students to touch it.

After interest slows, call the group back to the meeting area on the floor, or pick up the trays temporarily. (They won't hear you if the crabs are still in front of them.) You can hold a wrap-up discussion on how a crab pot works, the crab life cycle and habitat, and how to conduct the crab dissection.

DISSECTION PROCEDURE

Don't be intimidated by dissection. Once students have permission, they'll handle most of it themselves. Some groups stay engaged with just discussions and external examinations, so you may not need or want to dissect. *Dissecting is up to the facilitator.* An alternative to a class dissection is the teacher dissecting a single specimen as a demonstration.

Each group should remove and examine the crab's legs (pull and twist). Next, turn the crab onto its back. Pry up the abdomen, which looks like a tail, and break it off. Once it is lifted, it should snap off easily. Turn the crab up onto its face, and push your thumbs between the carapace (top shell) and the rest of the body. The body is like a small army tank, so be prepared to use some force. *This isn't a delicate, fingertip operation.*

With your thumbs in place, pull the carapace off the crab's body. Sometimes if a group is stuck, I partially lift the carapace to get them started. This will expose the internal structures. The feathery finger structures are the easiest to find. They are the gills. The yellow/brown material is a digestive gland called the HEPATOPANCREAS. It's like the liver for purifying their blood, and it also helps break down a crab's food during digestion. In a restaurant, it's called mustard, and many folks like to eat it because of its rich flavor. Sometimes the heart is visible right in the middle, a little bit toward the back of the crab. If there is time remaining to look inside the legs, use pliers or a small hammer to crack the exoskeleton.

Conclusion/Cleanup

Students will ask to keep a piece of crab. They shouldn't do that. While it would be cool, these specimens will soon stink so bad that they'd have to throw them out, and their parents would be mad about the torturous stench. If someone insists, then they need parent permission and a place to leave the specimens outside to dry for several weeks.

At the end of the lab, tools and pans will need to be wiped and dried. *Only clean, dry tools and pans should be put away*—nothing wet, smeary, or crusty. If you used a cooler, leaving the lid open will allow it to air dry without stinking.

Specimens should only be saved if you have another lab on the same day. Otherwise, *throw them out!*

Crabby trash should not be left in the trashcan unless you really hate the janitor *and* the other teachers in your hallway. In that case, be sure to plan this activity for a Friday afternoon, and turn on the heat before you leave. You'll end up explaining yourself in the office Monday morning, but you'll be famous, and your peers will respect your stinky superpowers forever.

Pro tip: When your principal questions your sanity, you can use baking soda or fresh coffee grounds to absorb death smells. Sometimes I've sprinkled (poured) the grounds right on the carpet and vacuumed them up the next day.

INTERESTING FACTS

Crabs pee from a gland near their eyes.

Crabs are fierce hunters, and they are omnivores, cannibals, and scavengers.

A small crab can easily kill and eat a large crab if the large crab just molted and has a soft shell.

A male crab will protect his mate when her shell is soft during mating. He sits on her head, watching for danger, until her shell is hard again.

A blue crab with red on the tips of its claws is often a female. Some people think it looks like the crab painted her fingernails.

When it's time to molt, the crab's exoskeleton splits in the back, and the crab backs out of it. Once they are out, they take in water to swell their body to a larger size so that when their shell hardens, it will be big.

Crabs have hairy legs! Each hair is a touch sensor that lets them feel through their shell.

It's difficult to tell how old a crab is. Good diet and comfortable climate makes a larger crab, so size doesn't align with age. (Nine inches across seems to be the maximum size for a blue crab.) Each time a crab molts, it loses its "age record." There is, however, one section of the crab's eye that doesn't come off during molting. If you slice it and look at it under a microscope, it has rings like a tree trunk. Counting the rings will give you the crab's age. This only works with crabs that are willing to wear an eye patch, though, because you have to remove their eye.

Crab pots are so efficient at catching things that they pose a real danger to the environment if they are lost or abandoned. When a pot is lost, the bait attracts crabs and fish inside where they become trapped. When they die, they become the new bait to attract new crabs and fish, which eventually die and repeat the cycle. These crab-pot "zombies" can keep on catching for years. In areas where the crab population has gone down, states sometimes will pay fishermen to hunt for old crab pots instead of for crabs. When fishermen work to clear out the zombie pots, the crab population soon shows improvement.

It's possible to catch crabs without a crab pot: Tie a chicken leg onto a string, and cast it out in the water. As crabs find the bait, they'll tug at it as they try to scurry away with it. Slowly pull in the line until they are close enough to slip a net under them. You may be able to lift them from the water, but they'll only hold on for half a second before they drop off, so you have to be quick!

When you eat blue crabs for dinner, there is no blue in sight. A live blue crab's exoskeleton is very colorful, including the blue in its name. When the crab is cooked, the heat destroys most of the colors, leaving the bright red behind. The same color change happens when cooking lobsters and crayfish.

Exploring buoyancy, density, and volume
with the engineering process!

Foil-Boat Engineering

● ● ●

NEED HELP WITH THIS LAB? *Ask me!* Find me on Twitter: @ TheFort_FW. Remember to tag your photos with #TSCHB so we can see what's going on in your lab!

Caution: Water makes tile floors slippery! Be careful, or use carpeted floors.

BACKGROUND

Materials that are denser will *sink* in materials that are less dense. They have more mass/weight so gravity pulls them more. Keys sink in the pool, metal spoons sink into the bowl of milk, and heavy weight belts pull scuba divers to the bottom of the ocean.

Materials that are *less* dense will *float* on top of denser materials. Oil floats on water, helium floats in air, and life jackets hold people up in a swimming pool.

If an object floats, you can say that it is POSITIVELY BUOYANT. If it sinks, you would say that it is NEGATIVELY BUOYANT. You may also see objects that don't sink or float but rather hover in the middle of the water column. In that case, they are NEUTRALLY BUOYANT. A good example is a fish that adjusts its air bladder so that it doesn't float or sink. See "Neutral Buoyancy at the Dinner Table" at the end of the lab for a little mealtime science!

Sometimes objects made of materials denser than water will still float because of their shape. Imagine a battleship made of steel and concrete and weighing over one hundred thousand tons. Steel and concrete both sink in water, but because the ship is shaped like a bowl filled with air, it will float. Air is lighter than water, so a ship filled with air floats. If you get a hole in the ship, water flows in and pushes the air out, and the ship will sink.

When a boat floats, it presses into the water, pushing some water out of the way. The science word for that is *displace* or *displacement*. The water that is displaced weighs the *exact same amount* as the boat and the cargo in it.

Density in simplest terms is the amount of weight per unit of volume. (Yes, high school teachers, *mass* would be more precise than *weight*, but if you already understand that, you don't need this background info.) If you need more information about the difference between mass and weight, see *The Real Deal with Mass and Weight* at the end of this lab.

Gravity is the force that pulls all things with mass together. The larger the mass, the stronger the pull. Earth is larger than the objects around you, so the pull of the Earth's gravity is stronger than the gravity of those objects. They are still pulling on you, though. The moon's gravity is strong enough to pull up bulges in the oceans on Earth. Those bulges are the tides.

In today's lab, we will be using a *five-step engineering process*. The steps are:

1. Designing and planning.
2. Building.
3. Testing what works and doesn't work.

4. Improving your idea.

5. Repeat.

Don't mistake these steps for a checklist that ends at step 5. Instead, imagine an arrow from step 5 leading right back to the top of the list. Ideas and products created during the engineering process can *always* be improved upon. Students who say, "I'm finished!" have jumped out of the process. They need to jump back in and focus on how their design can be improved. This will encourage kids who discover that their first ideas don't work. The process is ongoing, so their design will continue to improve! This process also helps students focus on design instead of competing with other kids. Competition is great, but it can be distracting or frustrating if your group has wide-ranging ages and skills.

MATERIALS

You can use a roll of aluminum foil or precut sheets. Figure about three feet per student (one foot at a time). If you have a large group, it's easier to use precut foil. If your grocery store doesn't have it, Amazon, Costco, or a restaurant-supply store will.

You'll need one tank per pair or trio of students. They need to be big enough to hold about three inches of water and small enough to carry to the sink for filling and emptying. Fill tanks with water before welcoming in the group. I've used the same set of plastic shoe boxes for over ten years. You might want to just invest in a set from the dollar store.

You'll also need some small weights to put into the boats to test how much weight they can hold. You can use marbles, but twenty dollars in pennies is cheaper, and it's good for a normal-sized class.

If you use pennies, you get your money back at the end of the lab (or at least most of it).

Allocate one drying towel per water tank, plus a few extra for spills. The ones for drying off cars work great. Lay them on the table like a place mat, and place the tank right on top so the towel catches stray drips. Paper towels don't work—you *will* run out.

- Aluminum foil
- Tanks for holding water
- Pennies or marbles to be weights for testing the boats
- Bowls for holding the weights
- Drying cloths/absorbent towels

OPTIONAL

- Mop
- Scissors
- Water pitcher

SUGGESTED TIMING FOR ONE-HOUR LAB
(This is a framework; adjust as needed.)

- Ten minutes: arrival and show-and-tell
- Ten minutes: meeting on background information, engineering process, concepts, and supply and tool orientation
- Fifteen minutes: building and testing (if students are deeply engaged, make this first build longer)
- Five minutes: meeting on lessons learned, "I noticed/I wonder" statements, and questions

- Fifteen minutes: second build time
- Five minutes: cleanup (scraps in pile, pennies and boats out of the tanks, supplies collected and stacked, and tables dried)

BEHAVIOR EXPECTATIONS

- Keep wet foil, hands, and weights above the towels so the water won't spread.
- Walk. Running on wet floors will break your arm or crack your skull.
- This is Science Club, not swim team. Focus on building, not splashing.
- When your boat finally sinks, it becomes a bowl of water. When you pick up the boat, pour the water back into the tank. Don't set the boat full of water on the table because it will leak everywhere.
- Roll up sleeves.

CONCEPTS

- Low-density materials float in high-density materials.
- High-density materials can also float if you shape them correctly.
- Volume is the amount of space that an object takes up.

PROCEDURE

Have students gather in a whole group. Explain that they will be studying PHYSICS (the science of how things move). We will also use the engineering processes (design, build, test, and improve). Students will design and test their own boats made of foil to see how much weight their design will hold. After testing, they will improve their design so that it can hold more weight than before.

Students have total design freedom. They can fold, crease, mold, wrinkle, tear, and so on. This is not a competition between students, because that would stop people from trying risky or cool designs. Rather, students will use the engineering process to improve their design. Sometimes kids worry about "doing it wrong" because they have never built a boat before. Reassure them that "not knowing" is the point of the lab. Without the knowledge to build a boat, they will have to engineer a creative solution. With this freedom they can experiment with different designs that they would likely avoid if they were already an expert boat builder.

Safety is important, so students will keep *all* wet things on or above the towels. This includes wet foil, pennies, boats, and hands. They can stand at their station, but they need to stay at their spot.

Students will share tanks in groups of two or three. They each get their own foil sheet (one per student) to build with. Hand out the foil (about one foot each if using a roll). As students get their foil, they can walk to their station to begin the first build time.

Teacher quote of the day: "I give foil to kids who are sitting patiently."

After fifteen minutes of build time (or when most groups have exhausted their foil), gather back into a whole group to discuss what ideas worked and which ones were challenging. Students can share one at a time with the group, or if you have a giant collection of waving hands, have everyone share their observations with the two classmates sitting closest to them.

This meeting is a great time for consulting the group with some questions:

* Why do some objects float, while others sink?
* Why did some boats hold lots of weight, while others sank quickly?
* If a penny that is really small sinks, how does a giant battleship float?

After discussions, give students a new foil and let them have a second chance to build and test.

Begin cleaning up five minutes before dismissal. Have students put *all* pennies back in bowls and push all trash to the middle of the table. If another group is coming in afterward, replace or wring out the soaked towels, and throw away the trash.

Tips

* If providing an extra foil prevents a meltdown or would really motivate a student, it's better to give him or her an extra.
* If a student has to leave early and/or really loves the activity, send him or her home with a couple sheets of foil to build at home.

Interesting Facts

In ancient China, an emperor's young son weighed an elephant using buoyancy and displacement. The emperor's wise men couldn't figure out how to weigh an elephant, but the child prodigy figured it out. He found a boat large enough to hold the elephant and loaded the elephant into it. With the boat low in the water, he marked the side of the boat at the waterline. When he unloaded the elephant, the boat rose higher in the water. The boy then loaded the boat with stones until the mark was pushed back down to the waterline. He added up the weights of all the stones, and their weight was equal to the elephant's weight! The boy's name was Cao Chong, and his father was Cao Cao, if you'd like to look them up.

Displacement and negative buoyancy also have a starring role in "The Crow and the Pitcher" (one of Aesop's Fables). In the story, a thirsty crow finds a heavy pitcher with water down in the bottom. With the water out of reach, the crow discovers that dropping stones into the pitcher will displace the water, pushing it higher and higher until he could reach the water and get a drink. (Birds have been observed using that trick in real life, so *birdbrain* may be more of a complement than an insult.)

Oil, gasoline, and jet fuel all have a lower density than water. A jet airliner with full fuel tanks weighs many more tons than a plane with empty tanks, but the full plane can still float on water because of water's high density. Imagine a large gasoline tanker truck driving across a frozen lake and then crashing through a weak spot in the ice. Even though it weighs many tons, the truck would still float because of the lower density of the gasoline inside! That large volume of gasoline is less dense that the same volume of water that it displaces, so it floats! (This sort of traffic accident has happened more than a few times in areas where tanker trucks drive over frozen lakes.)

The Real Deal with Mass and Weight

The terms MASS and WEIGHT have enough in common that they are sometimes used interchangeably. They are pretty different, though. Mass *is the amount of matter* (atoms) that an object has in it. Weight *is the measure of gravity's pull on those atoms* (measurable with a scale).

The confusion happens because we all live on planet Earth, and our experience tells us that an object's weight is always the same (wrong). If you weigh a fifty-gram mass on a balance or a scale, our experience tells us that it *always* weighs fifty grams. It doesn't. Weight changes when you leave planet Earth. The fifty-gram mass can weigh much more or much less, depending on where you land your spaceship. (Fifty grams equals ten nickel coins.)

If you land on:	The fifty-gram mass weighs:
Earth's moon	8 grams
Mars	19 grams
International Space Station	0 grams (decimal is too small to fit here!)
Jupiter	118 grams
Pluto (not a planet, sorry)	3 grams
Jupiter's moon (Europa)	7 grams
Our sun (bring insulated boots)	1,357 grams

If you land on a neutron star, bring your spatula to scrape up the flattened nickels (and yourself). Those 10 nickels would weigh 7,000,000,000,000 grams! That's the same weight as 40 *billion* nickels on Earth. The constant change can drive scientists nuts! Thankfully, mass (the amount of material an object has in it) doesn't change when you end up on another planet. Mass can be measured on a balance as long as you can measure against a mass you already know (like the weights on a triple-beam balance).

Neutral Buoyancy at the Dinner Table

Next time you're at dinner, see if you can grab a piece of *raw* carrot off somebody's plate. (Baby carrots or slices work great, but shredded carrots not so much.) Find a small glass of water, drop your carrot in, and watch it sink to the bottom. Raw carrots are *denser* than water, but just barely. Next, grab the salt shaker, and start putting a pinch at a time into the water. Don't stir. You want the water to get *really* salty. (If you use a big glass, you'll run out of salt before it is salty enough.) As the salt dissolves in the water, it will make the water denser and denser. Eventually the water will be more dense than the carrot, and the carrot will lift off the bottom and begin to rise with each pinch of salt. If you stop adding while the carrot is in the middle of the glass, the carrot will be neutrally buoyant, and it will hover in the middle of the glass! (You can do the same trick with a whole raw egg, but carrots are easier.)

Conclusion

● ● ●

THANK YOU FOR READING *THE Science Club Handbook*! Hopefully you have found the tools and resources that you will need to create and nurture your own science club. Implementing these strategies has the potential to alter your professional path for the better, and I have every confidence that you, your students, and your peers will benefit from the process. As you transform and grow, please remember to make keen observations of the changes you make and the influence they have within your sphere. (And remember to share the fun on social media with the hashtag #TSCHB so we can connect all of our science-club experiences with each other!) If you track your constant progress, you'll go to bed one night as a regular teacher, and wake up the next morning ready to pack your unique experiences into a time machine and launch them into the future to help friends whom you haven't even met yet.

This book is my time machine, and you are my future friend. Writing *The Science Club Handbook* has been even more satisfying than I imagined it would be. The writing process has taken twelve months, and you, dear reader, have been on my mind daily for the entire year. I encourage you to connect with me anytime. I know the excitement, pressures, and stresses that educators work in, and we can all benefit from a support network of like-minded people.

If you ever need further background information for the strategies within this book, if your school needs help putting your club or your lessons together, or if you would like to chase big teacher dreams together, please reach out to me. I'm always looking for an adventure.